# Gospel of Life Prayer Cycle

*PRAY   STUDY   ACT   LOVE*

Compiled by Stephen Joseph Wolf

Copyright © 2007
Stephen Joseph Wolf
All Rights reserved.
No part of this book may be reproduced in any form without permission in writing from the publisher, except for the inclusion of brief quotations in a review, and except for the *Spiritual Adoption in the Gospel of Life* prayer (page 2) which may be used freely.

Gospel of Life Prayer Cycle includes seven excerpts from the Encyclical Letter given on March 25, 1995, the Solemnity of the Annunciation of the Lord, in the seventeenth year of the Pontificate of John Paul II, addressed to clergy, *religious, lay faithful, and all people of good will on the value and inviolability of human life: The Gospel of Life (Evangelium Vitae),* copyright protected by Libreria Editrice Vaticana.

The Scripture quotations contained herein are from the *New Revised Standard Version Bible: Catholic Edition* copyright © 1993 and 1989 by the Division of Christian Education of the National Council of the Churches of Christ in the U.S.A. Used with permission. All Rights Reserved.

The *Spiritual Adoption in the Gospel of Life* prayer was inspired by a short prayer attributed to Bishop Fulton Sheen, used at neighboring Holy Rosary Church. The *Spiritual Adoption in the Gospel of Life* is prayed at the conclusion of the Prayers of the Faithful at St. Stephen Catholic Community, in lieu of seasonal prayers for vocations, on six *Gospel of Life Sundays*. Used with permission. Songs are offered with apologies to real musicians. The cover photographs are by the compiler.

The publisher (idjc press) may be contacted at steve@idjc.info.

Additional copies are available from
St. Mary's Bookstore in Nashville, Tennessee
www.stmarysbookstore.com

Dedicated with gratitude to

Pope John Paul II,

Joseph Cardinal Bernardin,

and the Gospel Of Life Team of
Saint Stephen Catholic Community.




**Gospel of Life Prayer Cycle**
is inspired by the Liturgy of the Hours psalter,
various ritual mass readings for peace and justice,
the encyclical *The Gospel of Life (Evangelium Vitae)*
by Pope John Paul II, 1995, Cardinal Bernardin's
teaching on the consistent ethic, and hunger for
scripture manifested by parishioners.

The excerpts from Pope John Paul II's encyclical
*The Gospel of Life* are from paragraphs 99 (see page
4 here), 56 (see pg. 34), 105 (pg. 54), 98 (pg. 90),
70 (pg. 110), 81 (pg. 120), and 60 (see page 121).
But please read all 105 paragraphs.
Purchase a copy at any excellent bookstore
or find it on the vatican web site:
http://www.vatican.va/edocs/ENG0141/_INDEX.HTM.

**Jan: The Adoption Option**
Psalm 103   Genesis 2:4b-9,15
Psalm 33   Psalm 145   Mark 3:31-35

**Feb: Health Care With Dignity**
Psalm 102   Isaiah 35:1-10   Psalm 10:1-6,12-14
2 Corinthians 9:6-15   John 15:9-17   Matthew 15:29-31

**Mar: Nonviolence of Jesus**
Psalm 27   Genesis 4:3-6,abridged   Psalm 25
Romans 12:17-21   Psalm 85   Matthew 5:38-48

**Apr: God's Good Earth**
Psalm 19   Genesis 1:26-2:3   Daniel 3:57-90
Isaiah 45:18-25   Psalm 65   Mark 4:26-29

**May: Work That Works**
Psalm 34   Deuteronomy 8:6-20   Isaiah 61
Numbers 6:22-27   Psalm 112   Matthew 16:24-27

**Jun: Being Sexual Beings**
Psalm 63:1-8   Ephesians 4:30-5:2   Song of Songs 3:1-5
1 Corinthians 7:7-8   Psalm 117   John 15:12-17

**Jul: Freedom of Religion**
Psalm 67   James 3:13-18
Psalm 40   Psalm 84   Luke 4:16-22

**Aug: Food, Clothing and Shelter**
Isaiah 58:6-11   Deuteronomy 10:12-20a   Psalm 73
Job 31:16-28a   Psalm 96   Matthew 25:31-40

**Sep: Education**
Psalm 71   1 Kings 3:11-14   Wisdom 9:1-6,9-11
Deuteronomy 6:20-24   Psalm 104   Matthew 5:1-12

**Oct: Natural Dying**
Psalm 143:1-11   Romans 8:18-28   Psalm 91
James 5:13-16   Psalm 86   Luke 10:25-37

**Nov: World Peace**
Psalm 24   Isaiah 2:1-5   Isaiah 11:1-10   Psalm 82
Deuteronomy 30:15-19   Psalm 122   Mark 2:1-12

**Dec: Sabbath Rest**
Psalm 23   2 Chronicles 36:15-17a,19-21
Psalm 42   Psalm 146   1 Corinthians 11:23-26
Psalm 148   Mark 1:32-37

# GOSPEL OF LIFE PRAYER CYCLE

## CONTENTS

| | | |
|---|---|---|
| SPIRITUAL ADOPTION IN THE GOSPEL OF LIFE | | 2 |
| GOSPEL OF LIFE STUDY MEETING | | 3 |
| JAN | THE ADOPTION OPTION<br>responding to abortion | 5 |
| FEB | HEALTH CARE WITH DIGNITY<br>limited access to a human right | 15 |
| MAR | NONVIOLENCE OF JESUS<br>death penalty temptation | 25 |
| APR | GOD'S GOOD EARTH<br>responding to pollution | 35 |
| MAY | WORK THAT WORKS<br>living wage for the working poor | 45 |
| JUN | BEING SEXUAL BEINGS<br>dealing with the fire | 55 |
| JUL | FREEDOM OF RELIGION<br>the american experiment | 61 |
| AUG | FOOD, CLOTHING AND SHELTER<br>widows, aliens and orphans | 69 |
| SEP | EDUCATION<br>the right that can be the key | 79 |
| OCT | NATURAL DYING<br>resisting suicide assistance | 91 |
| NOV | WORLD PEACE<br>peoples at war | 101 |
| DEC | SABBATH REST<br>the right to trust in God | 111 |
| A KEY QUESTION? | | 121 |
| PONDER PAGES | | 122 |

PRAY    STUDY    ACT    LOVE

## SPIRITUAL ADOPTION IN THE GOSPEL OF LIFE

*L*iving God of Israel,
Christ, Son of the living God,
Holy Spirit, Advocate,
One God with many names,
I lift up to you this year
one unborn child at risk,
one newborn needing care,
one mother afraid or confused,
one father with faltering courage,
one aging sage in poor health,
one human alive on death row,
one victim of violence or torture,
one civilian in the crossfire of war,
one keeper of peace in danger,
one man wrestling with prejudice,
one woman in need of a neighbor,
one hard worker who is still poor,
one migrant worker seeking dignity,
one teen needing encouragement,
one child having difficulty learning,
one family lacking good health care,
one community suffering pollution,
and one in need of your grace.
*A*s you made each in your image,
so you call us to grow
into the likeness of the Risen Christ.
*L*et each day of this year bring
an advent of hope,
a new nativity of faith,
lenten solidarity of love,
the new way of easter joy,
and your abiding pentecost presence.
*A*s you have called me by name, and
I am yours, so do I adopt them in prayer
and beg you grant what you know they need
to have life and to the full.   *A*men.

# Gospel of Life Study Meeting

*A POSSIBLE SCHEDULE*

| | | |
|---|---|---|
| 7:00 PM | (5 MIN.) | **Gospel of Life Concerns** (what's going on?) |
| 7:05 PM | (15 MIN.) | **Prayer and Silence** (GOL prayer cycle) |
| 7:20 PM | (20 MIN.) | **Teaching** (team taking turns) |
| 7:40 PM | (5 MIN.) | **Break** |
| 7:45 PM | (25 MIN.) | **Reflection and Questions** (seeking to understand) |
| 8:10 PM | (15 MIN.) | **Act Question** (what are we being called to do?) |
| 8:25 PM | (5 MIN.) | **Intercessions and Closing Prayer** (spiritual adoption) |
| 8:30 PM | | **Adjourn** (sleep well) |

PRAY    STUDY    ACT    LOVE

In transforming culture so that it supports life,
*women* occupy a place, in thought and action,
which is unique and decisive.
It depends on them to promote a "new feminism"
which rejects the temptation of imitating models
of "male domination", in order to acknowledge
and affirm the true genius of women
in every aspect of the life of society, and
overcome all discrimination, violence and exploitation…

…I would now like to say a special word
to *women who have had an abortion.*
The Church is aware of the many factors
which may have influenced your decision,
and she does not doubt that in many cases
it was a painful and even shattering decision.
The wound in your heart may not yet have healed.
Certainly what happened was and remains terribly wrong.
But do not give in to discouragement and do not lose hope.
Try rather to understand what happened and face it honestly.
If you have not already done so,
give yourselves over with humility and trust to repentance.
The Father of mercies is ready to give you his forgiveness
and his peace in the Sacrament of Reconciliation.
You will come to understand that nothing is definitively lost
and you will also be able to ask forgiveness from your child,
who is now living in the Lord.
With the friendly and expert help and advice of other people,
and as a result of your own painful experience,
you can be among the most eloquent defenders
of everyone's right to life.
Through your commitment to life,
whether by accepting the birth of other children
or by welcoming and caring for those most in need of
someone to be close to them, you will become promoters
of a new way of looking at human life.

*Note: This word is also helpful to fathers.*

<u>The Gospel of Life</u> (*Evangelium Vitae*), Pope John Paul II, 1995, #99

**JANUARY**

# THE ADOPTION OPTION

responding to abortion

How Can I Keep From Singing

ENDLESS SONG

1. My life flows on in end-less song; A-bove earth's lam-en-ta-tion.
2. What though my joys and com-forts fade The Lord my Sa-vior liv-eth;
3. I lift my eyes; the clouds grow thin; I see the blue a-bove it;

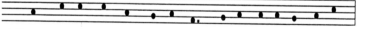

1. I hear that near and far-off hymn, It hails a new cre-a-tion:
2. What though the sha-dows ga-ther round Songs in the night he giv-eth:
3. And day by day clears way the path Since first I learned to love it:

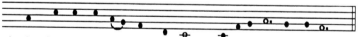

1. Through all the tu-mult and the strife I hear that mu-sic ring-ing;
2. No storm can shake my in-most calm, While to that ref-uge cling-ing;
3. The peace of Christ make fresh my heart, A foun-tain ev-er spring-ing;

1. It finds an ech-o_ in my soul; How can I keep from sing-ing?
2. Since Christ is Lord of_ heav'n and earth, How can I keep from sing-ing?
3. All things are mine since_ I am his; How can I keep from sing-ing?

Text: Robert Lowry, 1826-1899, 1860, altered

Music: 87 87, ENDLESS SONG, Quaker Hymn; Robert Lowry, altered

*Neither do I condemn you.*

Jesus of Nazareth, John 8:11b

## OPENING PRAYER

Leader: + O God, come to my assistance,

All: O Lord, make haste to help me.

Leader: Glory to the Father, and to the Son, and to the Holy Spirit,

All: As it was in the beginning, is now, and will be for ever. Amen.

## PSALM 103

Leader: Bless the Lord my soul; never forget all the Lord has done for you.

*Side 1 (Leader's Side)*
Bless the Lord, O my soul,
and all that is within me,
bless his holy name.
Bless the Lord, O my soul,
and do not forget all his benefits.

*Side 2*
Who forgives all your iniquity,
who heals all your diseases,
who redeems your life from the Pit,
who crowns you
with steadfast love and mercy,
who satisfies you with good
as long as you live
so that your youth
is renewed like the eagle's.

Side 1
The Lord works vindication,
justice for all who are oppressed.
He made known his ways to Moses,
his acts to the people of Israel.

Side 2
The Lord is merciful and gracious,
slow to anger
and abounding in steadfast love.
He will not always accuse,
nor will he keep his anger forever.
He does not deal with us
according to our sins,
nor repay us according to our iniquities.

Side 1
For as the heavens
are high above the earth,
so great is his steadfast love
toward those who fear him;
as far as the east is from the west
so far he removes
our transgressions from us.

Side 2
As a father has compassion for his children,
so the Lord has compassion
for those who fear him.
For he knows how we were made;
he remembers that we are dust.

Side 1
As for mortals, their days are like grass;
they flourish like a flower of the field;
for the wind passes over it, and it is gone,
and its place knows it no more.

*Side 2*

But the steadfast love of the Lord
is from everlasting to everlasting
on those who fear him,
and his righteousness
to children's children,
to those who keep his covenant
and remember to do his commandments.

*Side 1*

The Lord has established
his throne in the heavens,
and his kingdom rules over all.
Bless the Lord, O you his angels,
you mighty ones who do his bidding,
obedient to his spoken word.

*Side 2*

Bless the Lord, all his hosts,
his ministers that do his will.
Bless the Lord, all his works,
in all places of his dominion.
Bless the Lord, O my soul.

*Side 1*

> Glory to the Father, and to the Son,
> and to the Holy Spirit,

*Side 2*

> As it was in the beginning, is now,
> and will be for ever. Amen.

*All*

Bless the Lord, my soul; never forget
all the Lord has done for you.

THE ADOPTION OPTION

## First Reading

Genesis 2:4b-9,15

Reader:   A reading from the book of Genesis.

In the day that the Lord God made the earth and the heavens, when no plant of the field was yet in the earth and no herb of the field had yet sprung up - for the Lord God had not caused it to rain upon the earth, and there was no one to till the ground; but a stream would rise from the earth, and water the whole face of the ground - then the Lord God formed man from the dust of the ground, and breathed into his nostrils the breath of life; and the man became a living being.  And the Lord God planted a garden in Eden, in the east; and there he put the man whom he had formed. Out of the ground the Lord God made to grow every tree that is pleasant to the sight and good for food, the tree of life also in the midst of the garden, and the tree of the knowledge of good and evil.  The Lord God took the man and put him in the garden of Eden to till it and keep it.

Reader:      The word of the Lord.
All:         Thanks be to God.


## Psalm 33

Leader:   The loyal heart will praise the Lord.

*Side 1 (Leader's Side)*
Rejoice in the Lord, O you righteous
Praise befits the upright.

                    Side 2
Praise the Lord with the lyre;
make melody to him
with the harp of ten strings.
Sing to him a new song;
play skillfully on the strings
with loud shouts.
                    Side 1
For the word of the Lord is upright,
and all his work is done in faithfulness.
He loves righteousness and justice;
the earth is full
of the steadfast love of the Lord.
                    Side 2
By the word of the Lord
the heavens were made,
and all their host
by the breath of his mouth.
He gathered the waters of the sea
as in a bottle;
he put the deeps in storehouses.
                    Side 1
Let all the earth fear the Lord;
let all the inhabitants of the world
stand in awe of him.
For he spoke, and it came to be;
he commanded, and it stood firm.
                    Side 2
The Lord brings the counsel of the nations
to nothing;
he frustrates the plans of the peoples;
The counsel of the Lord stands forever,
the thoughts of his heart
to all generations.
                    Side 1
Happy is the nation whose God is the Lord,
the people whom he has chosen
as his heritage.                    - -

# THE ADOPTION OPTION

The Lord looks down from heaven;
he sees all humankind.
>Side 2

From where he sits enthroned he watches
all the inhabitants of the earth -
he who fashions the hearts of them all,
and observes their deeds.
>Side 1

A king is not saved by his great army;
a warrior is not delivered
by his great strength.
The war horse is a vain hope for victory,
and by its great might it cannot save.
>Side 2

Truly the eye of the Lord
is on those who fear him,
on those who hope in his steadfast love,
to deliver their soul from death,
and to keep them alive in famine.
>Side 1

Our soul waits for the Lord;
he is our help and shield.
Our heart is glad in him,
because we trust in his holy name.
>Side 2

Let your steadfast love, O Lord, be upon us
even as we hope in you.
>Side 1

> Glory to the Father, and to the Son,
> and to the Holy Spirit,
>>Side 2
> As it was in the beginning, is now,
> and will be for ever. Amen.

>All

The loyal heart will praise the Lord.

## Psalm 145

Leader: Day after day I will bless you, Lord;
    I will tell of your marvelous deeds.

Side 1 (Leader's Side)

I will extol you, my God and King,
and bless your name forever and ever.

Side 2

Every day I will bless you,
and praise your name forever and ever.
Great is the Lord,
and greatly to be praised:
his greatness is unsearchable.

1

One generation
shall laud your works to another,
and shall declare your mighty acts.

2

On the glorious splendor of your majesty,
and on your wondrous works,
I will meditate.

1

The might of your awesome deeds
shall be proclaimed,
and I will declare your greatness.
They shall celebrate
the fame of your abundant goodness,
and shall sing aloud of your righteousness.

2

The Lord is gracious and merciful,
slow to anger
and abounding in steadfast love.
The Lord is good to all,
and his compassion
is over all that he has made.

1

All your works shall give thanks
to you, O Lord,
and all your faithful shall bless you.
They shall speak of the glory of your
kingdom, and tell of your power,

2

To make known to all people
your mighty deeds,
and the glorious splendor of your kingdom.
Your kingdom is an everlasting kingdom,
and your dominion endures
throughout all generations.

1

The Lord is faithful in all his words,
and gracious in all his deeds.
The Lord upholds all who are falling,
and raises up all who are bowed down.

2

The eyes of all look to you,
and you give them their food in due season.
You open your hand,
satisfying the desire of every living thing.

1

The Lord is just in all his ways,
and kind in all his doings.
The Lord is near to all who call on him,
to all who call on him in truth.

2

He fulfills the desire of all who fear him;
he also hears their cry, and saves them.
The Lord watches over all who love him,
but all the wicked he will destroy.

1

My mouth will speak the praise of the Lord,
and all flesh will bless his holy name
forever and ever.

>    2
> Glory to the Father, and to the Son,
> and to the Holy Spirit,
>    1
> As it was in the beginning, is now,
> and will be for ever. Amen.

All

Day after day I will bless you, Lord;
I will tell of your marvelous deeds.


## SECOND READING                     Mark 3:31-35

Reader:  A reading from the gospel of Mark.

Then his mother and his brothers came; and standing outside, they sent to him and called him. A crowd was sitting around him; and they said to him, "Your mother and your brothers and sisters are outside, asking for you." And he replied, "Who are my mother and my brothers?" And, looking at those who sat around him, he said, "Here are my mother and my brothers! Whoever does the will of God is my brother and sister and mother."

Reader:    The gospel of the Lord.
All:       Praise to you, Lord Jesus Christ.


*Pause for silence.*

**February**

# HEALTH CARE WITH DIGNITY

limited access to a human right

### Shepherd Of Souls

ST. AGNES

1. Shep- herd of souls, re-fresh and bless Your cho- sen pil - grim flock
2. Hun - gry and thirst - ty, hu - man, weak, As you would come and go:
3. We would not live by bread a - lone, But by your word of grace,
4. Be known to us in break- ing bread, But do not then de - part;
5. Lord, sup with us in love di - vine; Your bod - y and your blood,

1. With man - na in the wil - der - ness, With wa - ter from the rock.
2. Our souls the joys of heav - en seek Which from your pas - sion flow.
3. In strength of which we trav - el on To our a - bi - ding place.
4. Sav - ior, a - bide with us, and spread Your ta - ble in our heart.
5. That liv - ing bread, that heav'n- ly wine, Be our e - ter - nal food.

Text: James Montgomery, 1771-1854, altered
Music: C.M., ST. AGNES, John B. Dykes, 1823-1876, 1866

### Opening Prayer

Leader: + O God, come to my assistance,

All: O Lord, make haste to help me.

Leader: Glory to the Father, and to the Son, and to the Holy Spirit,

All: As it was in the beginning, is now, and will be for ever. Amen.

## Psalm 102

Leader:  You, O Lord, established the earth,
and the heavens are the work of
your hands.

### Side 1 (Leader's Side)

Hear my prayer, O Lord;
let my cry come to you.
Do not hide your face from me
in the day of my distress.
Incline your ear to me;
answer me speedily in the day when I call.

### Side 2

For my days pass away like smoke,
and my bones burn like a furnace.
My heart is stricken
and withered like grass;
I am too wasted to eat my bread.
Because of my loud groaning
my bones cling to my skin.

1

I am like an owl of the wilderness,
like a little owl of the waste places.
I lie awake;
I am like a lonely bird on the housetop.
All day long my enemies taunt me;
those who deride me
use my name for a curse.

2

For I eat ashes like bread,
and mingle tears with my drink,
because of your indignation and anger;
for you have lifted me up
and thrown me aside.
My days are like an evening shadow;
I wither away like grass.

### 1

But you, O Lord, are enthroned forever;
your name endures to all generations.
You will rise up
and have compassion on Zion,
for it is time to favor it;
the appointed time has come.
For your servants hold its stones dear,
and have pity on its dust.

### 2

The nations will fear the name of the Lord,
and all the kings of the earth your glory.
For the Lord will build up Zion;
he will appear in his glory.
He will regard the prayer of the destitute,
and will not despise their prayer.

### 1

Let this be recorded
for a generation to come,
so that a people yet unborn
may praise the Lord;
that he looked down from his holy height,
from heaven the Lord looked at the earth,
to hear the groans of the prisoners,
to set free those who were doomed to die;

### 2

So that the name of the Lord
may be declared in Zion,
and his praise in Jerusalem,
when peoples gather together,
and kingdoms to worship the Lord.

1

He has broken my strength in midcourse;
he has shortened my days.
"O my God," I say, "do not take me away
at the mid-point of my life,
you whose years endure
throughout all generations."

2

Long ago you laid
the foundation of the earth,
and the heavens are the work of your hands.
They will perish, but you endure;
they will all wear out like a garment.
You change them like clothing,
and they pass away;
but you are the same,
and your years have no end.

1

The children of your servants
shall live secure;
their offspring shall be established
in your presence.

2

> Glory to the Father, and to the Son,
> and to the Holy Spirit,

1

> As it was in the beginning, is now,
> and will be for ever.  Amen.

All

You, O Lord, established the earth,
and the heavens are the work of your hands.

HEALTH CARE WITH DIGNITY

## **FIRST READING**   Isaiah 35:1-10

Reader:   A reading from the book of the
          prophet Isaiah:

The wilderness and the dry land
shall be glad,
the desert shall rejoice and blossom;
like the crocus it shall blossom abundantly,
and rejoice with joy and singing.
The glory of Lebanon shall be given to it,
the majesty of Carmel and Sharon.
They shall see the glory of the Lord,
the majesty of our God.
Strengthen the weak hands,
and make firm the feeble knees.
Say to those who are of a fearful heart,
"Be strong, do not fear!  Here is your God.
He will come with vengeance,
with terrible recompense.
He will come and save you."
Then the eyes of the blind shall be opened,
and the ears of the deaf unstopped;
then the lame shall leap like a deer, and
the tongue of the speechless sing for joy.
For waters shall break forth
in the wilderness
and streams in the desert;
the burning sand shall become a pool,
and the thirsty ground springs of water;
The haunt of jackals shall become a swamp,
the grass shall become reeds and rushes.
A highway shall be there,
and it shall be called the Holy Way;
the unclean shall not travel on it,
but it shall be for God's people;
no traveler, not even fools, shall go astray.

No lion shall be there,
nor shall any ravenous beast come upon it;
they shall not be found there
but the redeemed shall walk there.
And the ransomed of the Lord shall return,
and come to Zion with singing;
everlasting joy shall be upon their heads;
they shall obtain joy and gladness,
and sorrow and sighing shall flee away.

Reader: The word of the Lord.
All: Thanks be to God.

## PSALM 10:1-6,12-14

Leader: The Lord is just; Our God will defend the poor.

1

Why, O Lord, do you stand far off?
Why do you hide yourself
in times of trouble?
In arrogance the wicked persecute the poor –
let them be caught in the schemes
they have devised.

2

For the wicked boast
of the desires of their heart,
those greedy for gain
curse and renounce the Lord.
In the pride of their countenance
the wicked say, "God will not seek it out;"
all their thoughts are, "There is no God."

1

Their ways prosper at all times;
your judgments are on high,
out of their sight;
as for their foes, they scoff at them.

HEALTH CARE WITH DIGNITY

      2
They think in their heart,
"We shall not be moved;
throughout all generations
we shall not meet adversity."
      1
Rise up, O Lord; O God, lift up your hand;
do not forget the oppressed.
Why do the wicked renounce God,
and say in their hearts,
"You will not call us to account"?
      2
But you do see!
Indeed you note trouble and grief,
that you may take it into your hands;
the helpless commit themselves to you;
you have been the helper of the orphan.

      1
> Glory to the Father, and to the Son,
> and to the Holy Spirit,
>
>      2
> As it was in the beginning, is now,
> and will be for ever. Amen.

      All
The Lord is just; Our God will defend
the poor.


## SECOND READING   2 Corinthians 9:6-15

Reader: A reading from the second letter to
    the Corinthians:

The point is this: the one who sows
sparingly will also reap sparingly, and

the one who sows bountifully will also reap bountifully. Each of you must give as you have made up your mind, not reluctantly or under compulsion, for God loves a cheerful giver. And God is able to provide you with every blessing in abundance, so that by always having enough of everything, you may share abundantly in every good work. As it is written, "He scatters abroad, he gives to the poor; his righteousness endures forever." He who supplies seed to the sower and bread for food will supply and multiply your seed for sowing and increase the harvest of your righteousness. You will be enriched in every way for your great generosity, which will produce thanksgiving to God through us; for the rendering of this ministry not only supplies the needs of the saints but also overflows with many thanksgivings to God. Through the testing of this ministry you glorify God by your obedience to the confession of the gospel of Christ and by the generosity of your sharing with them and with all others, while they long for you and pray for you because of the surpassing grace of God that he has given you. Thanks be to God for his indescribable gift!

Reader: The word of the Lord.
All: Thanks be to God.

## JOHN 15:9-17

Leader: I have called you friends.

Side 1 (Leader's Side)
As the Father has loved me
so I have loved you;
abide in my love.

Side 2
If you keep my commandments,
you will abide in my love,
just as I have kept
my Father's commandments
and abide in his love.

1
I have said these things to you
so that my joy may be in you,
and that your joy may be complete.

2
This is my commandment,
that you love one another
as I have loved you.

1
No one has greater love than this,
to lay down one's life for one's friends.
You are my friends
if you do what I command you.

2
I do not call you servants any longer,
because the servant does not know
what the master is doing;
but I have called you friends,
because I have made known to you
everything that I have heard
from my Father.

1
You did not choose me but I chose you.
And I appointed you to go and bear fruit,
fruit that will last,
so that the Father will give you
whatever you ask him in my name.

> 2
>
> I am giving you these commands
> so that you may love one another.
>
>> 1
>>
>> Glory to the Father, and to the Son,
>> and to the Holy Spirit,
>>
>> 2
>>
>> As it was in the beginning, is now,
>> and will be for ever. Amen.

> All
>
> I have called you friends.

## Third Reading

Matthew 15:29-31

Reader: A reading from the gospel of Matthew.

After Jesus had left that place, he passed along the Sea of Galilee, and he went up the mountain, where he sat down. Great crowds came to him, bringing with them the lame, the maimed, the blind, the mute, and many others. They put them at his feet, and he cured them, so that the crowd was amazed when they saw the mute speaking, the maimed whole, the lame walking, and the blind seeing. And they praised the God of Israel.

Reader: The gospel of the Lord.
All: Praise to you, Lord Jesus Christ.

*Pause for silence.*

## March

# NONVIOLENCE OF JESUS

death penalty temptation

There's A Wideness In God's Mercy

HYFRYDOL

1. There's a wide-ness in God's mer-cy    Like the wide-ness of__ the sea;
2. For the love of God is broad-er    Than the mea-sures of__ our mind,
3. Trou-bled souls, why will you scat-ter    Like a crowd of fright-ened sheep?

1. There's a kind-ness in God's jus-tice    Which is more than lib-er-ty.
2. And the heart of the E-ter-nal    Is most won-der-ful-ly kind.
3. Fool-ish hearts, why will you wan-der    From a love so true and deep?

1. There is plen-ti-ful re-demp-tion    In the blood that has been shed;
2. If our love were but more sim-ple    We might take him at his word,
3. There is wel-come for the sin-ner    And more grac-es for the good;

1. There is joy for all the mem-bers    In the sor-rows of the Head.
2. And our lives would be thanks-giv-ing    For the good-ness of our Lord.
3. There is mer-cy with the Sav-ior,    There is heal-ing in his blood.

Text: Frederick W. Faber, 1814-1863, altered

Music: 87 87 D. HYFRYDOL; Rowland H. Prichard, 1811-1887

Traditional Melody for: *Love Divine, All Love Excelling*

*God did not make death,*
*and he does not delight*
*in the death of the living.*

The Wisdom of Solomon 1:13

## Opening Prayer

Leader: + O God, come to my assistance,

All: O Lord, make haste to help me.

Leader: Glory to the Father, and to the Son,
and to the Holy Spirit,

All: As it was in the beginning, is now,
and will be for ever. Amen.

## Psalm 27

Leader: The Lord is my light and my help;
whom shall I fear?

*Side 1 (Leader's Side)*
The Lord is my light and my salvation;
whom shall I fear?
The Lord is the stronghold of my life;
of whom shall I be afraid?

*Side 2*
When evildoers assail me to devour my flesh
my adversaries and foes
they shall stumble and fall.

1

Though an army encamp against me,
my heart shall not fear;
though war rise up against me,
yet will I be confident.

2

One thing I ask of the Lord,
that will I seek after:
to live in the house of the Lord
all the days of my life, - -

to behold the beauty of the Lord,
and to inquire in his temple.

1

For he will hide me in his shelter
in the day of trouble;
he will conceal me
under the cover of his tent;
he will set me high on a rock.

2

Now my head is lifted up
above my enemies all around me,
and I will offer in his tent
sacrifices with shouts of joy;
I will sing and make melody to the Lord.

1

Hear, O Lord, when I cry aloud,
be gracious to me and answer me!
"Come," my heart says, "seek his face!"
Your face, Lord, do I seek.
Do not hide your face from me.

2

Do not turn your servant away in anger,
you who have been my help.
Do not cast me off, do not forsake me,
O God of my salvation!
If my father and mother forsake me,
the Lord will take me up.

1

Teach me your way, O Lord,
and lead me on a level path
because of my enemies.
Do not give me up
to the will of my adversaries,
for false witnesses have risen against me,
and they are breathing out violence.

> 2
I believe that I shall see
the goodness of the Lord
in the land of the living.
Wait for the Lord;
be strong, and let your heart take courage;
wait for the Lord!

> 1
> Glory to the Father, and to the Son,
> and to the Holy Spirit,
>
> 2
> As it was in the beginning, is now,
> and will be for ever.  Amen.

All
The Lord is my light and my help;
whom shall I fear?

## First Reading

Genesis 4:3-16 abridged

Reader:   A reading from the book of Genesis.

In the course of time Cain brought to
the Lord an offering of the fruit of the
ground, and Abel for his part brought of the
firstlings of his flock, their fat portions.
And the Lord had regard for Abel and his
offering, but for Cain and his offering
he had no regard.  So Cain was very angry,
and his countenance fell.  The Lord said to
Cain, "Why are you angry, and why has your
countenance fallen?  If you do well, will
you not be accepted?  And if you do not
do well, sin is lurking at the door; its
desire is for you, but you must master it."
Cain said to his brother Abel, "Let us go
out to the field."  And when they were in
the field, Cain rose up against his brother

Abel, and killed him. Then the Lord said to Cain, "Where is your brother Abel?" He said, "I do not know; am I my brother's keeper?" And the Lord said, "What have you done? Listen; your brother's blood is crying out to me from the ground!...The ground which has received your brother's blood… will no longer yield to you its strength; you will be a fugitive and a wanderer on the earth." Cain said to the Lord, "My punishment is greater than I can bear!... Anyone who meets me may kill me." The Lord said, "Not so! Whoever kills Cain will suffer a sevenfold vengeance." And the Lord put a mark on Cain, so that no one who came upon him would kill him.

Reader: The word of the Lord.
All: Thanks be to God.

## PSALM 25

Leader: Guide me, O Lord, in your truth.

1

To you, O Lord, I lift up my soul.
O my God, in you I trust;
do not let me be put to shame;
do not let my enemies exult over me.
Do not let those who wait for you
be put to shame;
let them be ashamed
who are wantonly treacherous.

2

Make me know your ways, O Lord;
teach me your paths.
Lead me in your truth, and teach me,
for you are the God of my salvation;
for you I wait all day long.

1

Be mindful of your mercy, O Lord,
and of your steadfast love,
for they have been from of old.
Do not remember the sins of my youth
or my transgressions;
according to your steadfast love
remember me,
for your goodness' sake, O Lord!

2

Good and upright is the Lord;
therefore he instructs sinners in the way.
He leads the humble in what is right,
and teaches the humble his way.
All the paths of the Lord
are steadfast love and faithfulness,
for those who keep his covenant and decrees.

1

For your name's sake, O Lord,
pardon my guilt, for it is great.
Who are they that fear the Lord?
He will teach them the way
that they should choose.

2

They will abide in prosperity,
and their children shall possess the land.
The friendship of the Lord
is for those who fear him,
and he makes his covenant known to them.
My eyes are ever toward the Lord,
for he will pluck my feet out of the net.

1

Turn to me and be gracious to me,
for I am lonely and afflicted.
Relieve the troubles of my heart,
and bring me out of my distress.
Consider my affliction and my trouble,
and forgive all my sins.

2

Consider how many are my foes,
and with what violent hatred they hate me.
O guard my life, and deliver me;
do not let me be put to shame,
for I take refuge in you.
May integrity and uprightness preserve me,
for I wait for you.

1

Redeem Israel, O God,
out of all its troubles.

2

> Glory to the Father, and to the Son,
> and to the Holy Spirit,
>
> 1
>
> As it was in the beginning, is now,
> and will be for ever. Amen.

All

Guide me, O Lord, in your truth.

## SECOND READING           Romans 12:17-21

Reader:   A reading from the letter of Paul
          to the Romans

Do not repay anyone evil for evil, but
take thought for what is noble in the sight
of all. If it is possible, so far as it
depends on you, live peaceably with all.
Beloved, never avenge yourselves, but
leave room for the wrath of God; for it is
written, "Vengeance is mine, I will repay,
says the Lord." No, "if your enemies are
hungry, feed them; if they are thirsty,
give them something to drink; for by doing

this you will heap burning coals on their heads." Do not be overcome by evil, but overcome evil with good.

Reader: The word of the Lord.
All: Thanks be to God.

## Psalm 85

Leader: Mercy and faithfulness have met;
justice and peace have embraced.

1

Lord, you were favorable to your land;
you restored the fortunes of Jacob.
You forgave the iniquity of your people;
you pardoned all their sin.
You withdrew all your wrath;
you turned from your hot anger.

2

Restore us again, O God of our salvation,
and put away your indignation toward us.
Will you be angry with us forever?
Will you prolong your anger
to all generations?

1

Will you not revive us again,
so that your people may rejoice in you?
Show us your steadfast love, O Lord,
and grant us your salvation.

2

Let me hear what God the Lord will speak,
for he will speak peace to his people,
to his faithful,
to those who turn to him in their hearts.
Surely his salvation is at hand
for those who fear him,
that his glory may dwell in our land.

NONVIOLENCE OF JESUS

1

Steadfast love and faithfulness will meet;
righteousness and peace
will kiss each other.
Faithfulness will spring up from the ground,
and righteousness
will look down from the sky.

2

The Lord will give what is good,
and our land will yield its increase.
Righteousness will go before him,
and will make a path for his steps.

1

> Glory to the Father, and to the Son,
> and to the Holy Spirit,
>
> 2
>
> As it was in the beginning, is now,
> and will be for ever.  Amen.

All

Mercy and faithfulness have met;
justice and peace have embraced.


## THIRD READING

Matthew 5:38-48

Reader: A reading from the gospel of Matthew.

"You have heard it said, 'An eye for an eye
and a tooth for a tooth.'  But I say to you,
Do not resist an evildoer.  But if anyone
strikes you on the right cheek, turn the
other also; and if anyone wants to sue you
and take your coat, give your cloak as well;
and if anyone forces you to go one mile, go
also the second mile.  Give to everyone who
begs from you, and do not refuse anyone who
wants to borrow from you."

"You have heard it said, 'You shall love your neighbor and hate your enemy.' But I say to you, Love your enemies and pray for those who persecute you, so that you may be children of your Father in heaven; for he makes his sun rise on the evil and on the good, and sends rain on the righteous and on the unrighteous. For if you love those who love you, what reward do you have? Do not even the tax collectors do the same? And if you greet only your brothers and sisters, what more are you doing than the others? Do not even the Gentiles do the same? Be perfect, therefore, as your heavenly Father is perfect."

Reader: The gospel of the Lord.
All: Praise to you, Lord Jesus Christ.

*Pause for silence.*

**Punishment ought not go to
the extreme of executing the offender
except in cases of absolute necessity:
in other words,
when it would not be possible otherwise to defend society.
Today however, as a result of steady improvements
in the organization of the penal system,
such cases are very rare,
if not practically non-existent.**

The Gospel of Life (*Evangelium Vitae*), Pope John Paul II, 1995, #56

## April

# GOD'S GOOD EARTH

## responding to pollution

### For The Beauty Of The Earth

DIX

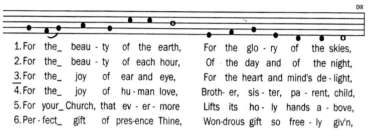

1. For the_ beau-ty of the earth, For the glo-ry of the skies,
2. For the_ beau-ty of each hour, Of the day and of the night,
3. For the_ joy of ear and eye, For the heart and mind's de-light,
4. For the_ joy of hu-man love, Broth-er, sis-ter, pa-rent, child,
5. For your_ Church, that ev-er-more Lifts its ho-ly hands a-bove,
6. Per-fect_ gift of pres-ence Thine, Won-drous gift so free-ly giv'n,

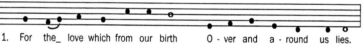

1. For the_ love which from our birth  O-ver and a-round us lies.
2. Hill and_ val-ley, tree and flow'r, Sun and moon and stars of light.
3. For the_ mys-tic har-mo-ny Link-ing sense to sound and sight.
4. Friends on_ earth and friends a-bove, Sin-gle, mar-ried, vir-gins mild.
5. Off-'ring_ up on ev-'ry shore Faith and sa-cri-fi-cial love.
6. Gra-ces_ hu-man and di-vine, Peace on earth and joy in heav'n.

1-6. Lord of all, to you we raise   This our song of grate-ful praise.

Text: *Lyra Eucharistica*, 1864; Folliot S. Pierpoint, 1835-1917, 1864, altered

Music: DIX, 77 77 77, Conrad Kocher, 1786-1872, 1838; adapted by William H. Monk, 1823-1899

*Praise be my Lord for our mother the Earth,*
*which sustains us and keeps us,*
*and yields diverse fruits,*
*and flowers of many colors, and grass.*

St. Francis of Assisi, *Canticle of the Sun*

## OPENING PRAYER

Leader: + O God, come to my assistance,

All: O Lord, make haste to help me.

Leader: Glory to the Father, and to the Son, and to the Holy Spirit,

All: As it was in the beginning, is now, and will be for ever. Amen.

## PSALM 19

Leader: The vaults of heaven ring with your praise, O Lord.

Side 1 (Leader's Side)
The heavens are telling the glory of God;
and the firmament proclaims his handiwork.
Day to day pours forth speech,
and night to night declares knowledge.

Side 2
There is no speech, nor are there words;
their voice is not heard;
yet their voice goes out
through all the earth,
and their words to the end of the world.

1
In the heavens he has set a tent for the sun
which comes out like a bridegroom
from his wedding canopy,
like a strong man runs its course with joy.

2
Its rising is from the end of the heavens,
and its circuit to the end of them;
and nothing is hid from its heat.

1
The law of the Lord is perfect,
reviving the soul;
the decrees of the Lord are sure,
making wise the simple;

2
The precepts of the Lord are right,
rejoicing the heart;
the commandment of the Lord is clear,
enlightening the eyes;

1
The fear of the Lord is pure,
enduring forever;
the ordinances of the Lord are true
and righteous altogether.

2
More to be desired are they than gold,
even much fine gold;
sweeter also than honey,
and drippings of the honeycomb.

1
Moreover by them is your servant warned;
in keeping them there is great reward.
But who can detect their errors?
Clear me from hidden faults.

2
Keep back your servant
also from the insolent;
do not let them have dominion over me.
Then I shall be blameless,
and innocent of great transgression.

1
Let the words of my mouth
and the meditation of my heart
be acceptable to you,
O Lord, my rock and my redeemer.

> 2
> Glory to the Father, and to the Son,
> and to the Holy Spirit,
> 1
> As it was in the beginning, is now,
> and will be for ever. Amen.

All
The vaults of heaven ring with your praise,
O Lord.

## FIRST READING
Genesis 1:26-2:3

Reader: A reading from the book of Genesis.

Then God said, "Let us make humankind (adam) in our image, according to our likeness; and let them have dominion over the fish of the sea, and over the birds of the air, and over the cattle, and over all the wild animals of the earth, and over every creeping thing that creeps upon the earth." So God created humankind in his image, in the image of God he created them; male and female he created them. God blessed them, and God said to them, "Be fruitful and multiply, and fill the earth and subdue it; and have dominion over the birds of the air and over every living thing that moves upon the earth." God said, "See, I have given you every plant yielding seed that is upon the face of all the earth, and every tree with seed in its fruit; you shall have them for food. And to every beast of the earth, and to every bird of the air, and to everything that creeps on the earth, everything that

GOD'S GOOD EARTH

has the breath of life, I have given every green plant for food." And it was so. God saw everything that he had made, and indeed, it was very good. And there was evening and there was morning, the sixth day. Thus the heavens and the earth were finished, and all their multitude. And on the seventh day God finished the work that he had done, and he rested on the seventh day from all the work that he had done. So God blessed the seventh day and hallowed it, because on it God rested from all the work that he had done in creation.

Reader: The word of the Lord.
All: Thanks be to God.

## DANIEL 3:57-90

Leader: To you, Lord, be highest glory and praise forever, alleluia.

1

Bless the Lord, all you works of the Lord;
sing praise to him
and highly exalt him forever.
Bless the Lord, you heavens;
Bless the Lord, you angels of the Lord;
Bless the Lord,
all you waters above the heavens;
Bless the Lord, all you powers of the Lord;
Bless the Lord, sun and moon;
Bless the Lord, stars of heaven.

2

Bless the Lord, all rain and dew;
Bless the Lord, all you winds;
Bless the Lord, fire and heat;
Bless the Lord, winter cold and summer heat;
Bless the Lord, dews and falling snow;
Bless the Lord, ice and cold;
Bless the Lord, frost and snows;
Bless the Lord, nights and days;
Bless the Lord, light and darkness;
Bless the Lord, lightnings and clouds.

1

Let the earth bless the Lord;
let it sing praise to him
and highly exalt him forever.
Bless the Lord, mountains and hills;
Bless the Lord, all that grows in the ground;
Bless the Lord, you springs;
Bless the Lord, seas and rivers;
Bless the Lord, you whales
and all that swims in the waters;
Bless the Lord, all birds of the air;
Bless the Lord, all wild animals and cattle;
Bless the Lord, all people on earth.

2

Bless the Lord, O Israel;
sing praise to him
and highly exalt him forever.
Bless the Lord, you priests of the Lord;
Bless the Lord, you servants of the Lord;
Bless the Lord,
spirits and souls of the righteous;
Bless the Lord,
you who are holy and humble in heart;
Bless the Lord
Hananiah, Azariah, and Mishael;
sing praise to him
and highly exalt him forever.

# GOD'S GOOD EARTH

1
Let us bless the Father, and the Son,
and the Holy Spirit.
sing praise to him
and highly exalt him forever.
Blessed are you in the firmament of heaven,
and to be sung and glorified forever.

All
To you, Lord, be highest glory and praise
forever, alleluia.

## SECOND READING

Isaiah 45:18-25

Reader: A reading from the book of the prophet Isaiah.

For thus says the Lord, who created the heavens (he is God!), who formed the earth and made it (he established it; he did not create it a chaos, he formed it to be inhabited!): I am the Lord and there is no other. I did not speak in secret, in a land of darkness; I did not say to the offspring of Jacob, "Seek me in chaos." I the Lord speak the truth, I declare what is right. Assemble yourselves and come together, draw near, you survivors of the nations! They have no knowledge - those who carry about their wooden idols, and keep on praying to a god that cannot save. Declare and present your case; let them take counsel together! Who told this long ago? Who declared it of old? Was it not I, the Lord? There is no other god besides me, a righteous God and a Savior; there is no one besides me. Turn to

me and be saved, all the ends of the earth!
For I am God, and there is no other. By
myself I have sworn, from my mouth has gone
forth in righteousness a word that shall not
return: "To me every knee shall bow, every
tongue shall swear." Only in the Lord, it
shall be said of me, are righteousness and
strength; all who were incensed against him
shall come to him and be ashamed. In the
Lord all the offspring of Israel shall
triumph and glory.

Reader: The word of the Lord.
All: Thanks be to God.

## PSALM 65

Leader: To you, O God, our praise is due in Zion.

1

Praise is due to you, O God, in Zion;
and to you shall vows be performed,
O you who answer prayer!

2

To you all flesh shall come.
When deeds of iniquity overwhelm us,
you forgive our transgressions.

1

Happy are those
whom you choose and bring near
to live in your courts.
We shall be satisfied with the goodness
of your house, your holy temple.

## GOD'S GOOD EARTH

2

By awesome deeds
you answer us with deliverance,
O God of our salvation;
you are the hope
of all the ends of the earth
and of the farthest seas.

1

By your strength
you established the mountains;
you are girded with might.
You silence the roaring of the seas,
the roaring of their waves,
the tumult of the peoples.

2

Those who live at earth's farthest bounds
are awed by your signs;
you make the gateways of the morning
and the evening shout for joy.

1

You visit the earth and water it,
you greatly enrich it;
the river of God is full of water;
you provide the people with grain,
for so you have prepared it.

2

You water its furrows abundantly,
settling its ridges,
softening it with showers,
and blessing its growth.

1

You crown the year with your bounty;
your wagon tracks overflow with richness.
The pastures of the wilderness overflow
the hills gird themselves with joy.

> 2
> The meadows clothe themselves with flocks,
> the valleys deck themselves with grain,
> they shout and sing together for joy.
>
>> 1
>> Glory to the Father, and to the Son,
>> and to the Holy Spirit,
>> 2
>> As it was in the beginning, is now,
>> and will be for ever. Amen.
>
> All
> To you, O God, our praise is due in Zion.

## THIRD READING          Mark 4:26-29

Reader: A reading from the gospel of Mark.

Jesus also said, "The kingdom of God is as if someone would scatter seed on the ground and would sleep and rise night and day, and the seed would sprout and grow, he does not know how. The earth produces of itself, first the stalk, then the head, then the full grain in the head. But when the grain is ripe, at once he goes in with his sickle, because the harvest has come."

Reader: The gospel of the Lord.
All: Praise to you, Lord Jesus Christ.

*Pause for silence.*

# May

# WORK THAT WORKS

## living wage for the working poor

### Our God, Our Help In Ages Past

ST. ANNE

1. Our God, our help in a-ges past, Our hope for years to come,
2. Be-neath the shad-ow of your throne Your saints have dwelt se-cure;
3. Be-fore the hills in or-der stood, Or earth re-ceived her frame,
4. A thou-sand a-ges in your sight Are like an eve-ning gone;
5. Time, like an ev-er roll-ing stream, Bears all our lives a-way;
6. O God, our help in a-ges past, Our hope for years to come,

1. Our shel-ter from the storm-y blast, And our e-ter-nal home.
2. Suf-fi-cient is your arm a-lone, And our de-fense is sure.
3. From ev-er-last-ing you are God, To end-less years the same.
4. Short as the watch that ends the night Be-fore the ris-ing sun.
5. They fly, for-got-ten, as a dream Dies at the op-'ning day.
6. Be now our guard while trou-bles last, And our e-ter-nal home.

Text: Based on Psalm 90:1,2,4, Isaac Watts, 1674-1748, *The Psalms of David*, 1719, altered

Music: C.M., 86 86, ST. ANNE, William Croft. 1678-1727. 1708, altered

## Opening Prayer

Leader: + O God, come to my assistance,

All: O Lord, make haste to help me.

Leader: Glory to the Father, and to the Son, and to the Holy Spirit,

All: As it was in the beginning, is now, and will be for ever. Amen.

## Psalm 34

Leader:  Look to the Lord and be enlightened.

*Side 1 (Leader's Side)*

I will bless the Lord at all times;
his praise shall continually be in my mouth.
My soul makes its boast in the Lord;
let the humble hear and be glad.

*Side 2*

O magnify the Lord with me,
and let us exalt his name together.
I sought the Lord, and he answered me,
and delivered me from all my fears.

*1*

Look to him and be radiant;
so your faces shall never be ashamed.
This poor soul cried,
and was heard by the Lord,
and was saved from every trouble.

*2*

The angel of the Lord encamps
around those who fear him,
and delivers them.
O taste and see that the Lord is good;
happy are those who take refuge in him.

*1*

O fear the Lord, you his holy ones,
for those who fear him have no want.
The young lions suffer want and hunger,
but those who seek the Lord
lack no good thing.

*2*

Come, O children, listen to me;
I will teach you the fear of the Lord.
Which of you desires life,
and covets many days to enjoy good?

1

Keep your tongue from evil,
and your lips from speaking deceit.
Depart from evil, and do good;
seek peace, and pursue it.

2

The eyes of the Lord are on the righteous,
and his ears are open to their cry.
The face of the Lord is against evildoers,
to cut off the remembrance of them
from the earth.

1

When the righteous cry for help,
the Lord hears,
and rescues them from all their troubles.
The Lord is near to the brokenhearted,
and saves the crushed in spirit.

2

Many are the afflictions of the righteous,
but the Lord rescues them from them all.
He keeps all their bones;
not one of them will be broken.

1

Evil brings death to the wicked,
and those who hate the righteous
will be condemned.
The Lord redeems the life of his servants;
none of those who take refuge in him
will be condemned.

2

> Glory to the Father, and to the Son,
> and to the Holy Spirit,
>
> 1
>
> As it was in the beginning, is now,
> and will be for ever.  Amen.

All

Look to the Lord and be enlightened.

## First Reading

Deuteronomuy 8:6-20

Reader: A reading from the book of Deuteronomy.

Therefore keep the commandments of the Lord your God, by walking in his ways and by fearing him. For the Lord your God is bringing you into a good land, a land with flowing streams, with springs and underground waters welling up in valleys and hills, a land of wheat and barley, of vines and fig trees and pomegranates, a land of olive trees and honey, a land where you may eat bread without scarcity, where you will lack nothing, a land whose stones are iron and from whose hills you may mine copper. You shall eat your fill and bless the Lord your God for the good land that he has given you. Take care that you do not forget the Lord your God, by failing to keep his commandments, his ordinances, and his statutes, which I am commanding you today. When you have eaten your fill and have built fine houses and live in them, and when your herds and flocks have multiplied, and your silver and gold is multiplied, and all that you have is multiplied, then do not exalt yourself, forgetting the Lord your God, who brought you out of the land of Egypt, out of the house of slavery, who led you through the great and terrible wilderness, an arid wasteland with poisonous snakes and scorpions. He made water flow for you from flint rock, and fed you in the wilderness with manna that your ancestors did not know, to humble you and to test you, and in the end to do you good. Do not say to yourself,

"My power and the might of my own hand have gotten me this wealth." But remember the Lord your God, for it is he who gives you power to get wealth, so that he may confirm his covenant that he swore to your ancestors, as he is doing today. If you do forget the Lord your God and follow other gods to serve and worship them, I solemnly warn you today that you shall surely perish. Like the nations that the Lord is destroying before you, so shall you perish, because you would not obey the voice of the Lord your God.

Reader: The word of the Lord.
All: Thanks be to God.

## Isaiah 61

Leader: The Lord loves justice.

1
The spirit of the Lord God is upon me,
because the Lord has anointed me;
he has sent me to bring
good news to the oppressed,
to bind up the brokenhearted,

2
To proclaim liberty to the captives,
and release to the prisoners;
to proclaim a year of the Lord's favor,
and days of vengeance of our God;
to comfort all who mourn;

1
To provide for those who mourn in Zion -
to give them a garland instead of ashes,
the oil of gladness instead of mourning,
a mantle of praise instead of a faint spirit.

They will be called oaks of righteousness,
the planting of the Lord,
to display his glory.

They shall build up the ancient ruins,
they shall raise up the former devastations;
they shall repair the ruined cities,
the devastations of many generations.

Strangers shall stand and feed your flocks,
foreigners shall till your land
and dress your vines.

But you shall be called priests of the Lord,
you shall be named ministers of our God;
you shall enjoy the wealth of the nations,
and in their riches you shall glory.

Because their shame was double,
and dishonor was proclaimed as their lot,
therefore they shall possess
a double portion;
everlasting joy shall be theirs.

For I the Lord love justice,
I hate robbery and wrongdoing;
I will faithfully give them
their recompense,
and I will make
an everlasting covenant with them.

Their descendants shall be known
among the nations,
and their offspring among the peoples;
all who see them shall acknowledge
that they are a people
whom the Lord has blessed.

1
I will greatly rejoice in the Lord,
my whole being shall exult in my God;
for he has clothed me
with the garments of salvation,
he has covered me
with the robe of righteousness,
as a bridegroom
decks himself with a garland,
and as a bride
adorns herself with her jewels.

2
For as the earth brings forth shoots,
and as a garden causes what is sown in it
to spring up,
so the Lord God will cause
righteousness and praise
to spring up before all the nations.

> 1
> Glory to the Father, and to the Son,
> and to the Holy Spirit,
>
> 2
> As it was in the beginning, is now,
> and will be for ever. Amen.

All
The Lord loves justice.


## SECOND READING        Numbers 6:22-27

Reader:    A reading from the book of Numbers.

The Lord spoke to Moses, saying: Speak to
Aaron and his sons, saying, Thus you shall
bless the Israelites: You shall say to them,

The Lord bless you and keep you;
the Lord make his face to shine upon you,
and be gracious to you;
the Lord lift up his countenance upon you,
and give you peace.
So they shall put my name on the Israelites,
and I will bless them.

Reader: The word of the Lord.
All: Thanks be to God.

## PSALM 112

Leader: Blessed are they who
hunger and thirst for holiness;
they will be satisfied.

1

Praise the Lord!
Happy are those who fear the Lord,
who greatly delight in his commandments.
Their descendants will be
mighty in the land;
the generation of the upright
will be blessed.

2

Wealth and riches are in their houses,
and their righteousness endures forever.
They rise in the darkness
as a light for the upright;
they are gracious, merciful and righteous.

1

It is well with those
who deal generously and lend,
who conduct their affairs with justice.
For the righteous will never be moved;
they will be remembered forever.

2
They are not afraid of evil tidings;
their hearts are firm, secure in the Lord.
Their hearts are steady,
they will not be afraid;
in the end they will look in triumph
on their foes.

1
They have distributed freely,
they have given to the poor;
their righteousness endures forever;
their horn is exalted in honor.

2
The wicked see it and are angry;
they gnash their teeth and melt away;
the desire of the wicked comes to nothing.

1
>    Glory to the Father, and to the Son,
>    and to the Holy Spirit,
> 
> 2
>    As it was in the beginning, is now,
>    and will be for ever.  Amen.

All
Blessed are they who hunger and thirst for holiness; they will be satisfied.


## THIRD READING
Matthew 16:24-27

Reader: A reading from the gospel of Matthew.

Then Jesus told his disciples, "If any want to become my followers, let them deny themselves and take up their cross and follow me.  For those who want to save their life will lose it, and those who lose their life for my sake will find it. For what will it profit them if they gain the whole world but forfeit their life? Or what will they give in return for their life? For the Son of Man is to come with his angels in the glory of his Father, and then he will repay everyone for what has been done."

Reader: The gospel of the Lord.
All: Praise to you, Lord Jesus Christ.

*Pause for silence.*

O Mary,
bright dawn of the new world,
Mother of the living,
to you do we entrust the cause of life:
Look down, O Mother,
upon the vast numbers of babies not allowed to be born,
of the poor whose lives are made difficult,
of men and women who are victims of brutal violence,
of the elderly and sick killed by indifference
or out of misguided mercy.
Grant that all who believe in your Son
may proclaim the Gospel of Life
with honesty and love to the people of our time.
Obtain for them the grace to accept that Gospel as a gift ever new
the joy of celebrating it with gratitude throughout their lives
and the courage to bear witness to it resolutely,
in order to build, together with all people of good will,
the civilization of truth and love,
to the praise and glory of God, the Creator and lover of life.

The Gospel of Life (*Evangelium Vitae*), Pope John Paul II, 1995, #105

# JUNE

# BEING SEXUAL BEINGS

## dealing with the fire

### Our Father, All Creating

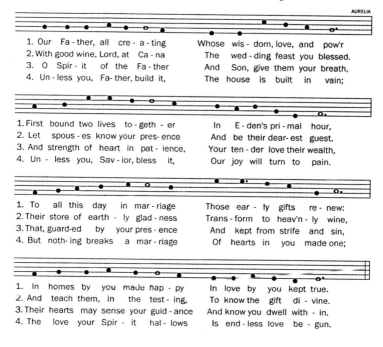

AURELIA

1. Our Father, all creating, Whose wisdom, love, and pow'r
First bound two lives together In Eden's primal hour,
To all this day in marriage Those early gifts renew:
In homes by you made happy In love by you kept true.

2. With good wine, Lord, at Cana The wedding feast you blessed.
Let spouses know your presence And be their dearest guest.
Their store of earthly gladness Transform to heav'nly wine,
And teach them, in the testing, To know the gift divine.

3. O Spirit of the Father And Son, give them your breath,
And strength of heart in patience, Your tender love their wealth,
That, guarded by your presence And kept from strife and sin,
Their hearts may sense your guidance And know you dwell within.

4. Unless you, Father, build it, The house is built in vain;
Unless you, Savior, bless it, Our joy will turn to pain.
But nothing breaks a marriage Of hearts in you made one;
The love your Spirit hallows Is endless love begun.

Text: John Ellerton, 1826-1893, altered significantly
Music: 76 76 D, AURELIA, Samuel S. Wesley, 1810-1876, 1864
Traditional Melody for: *The Church's One Foundation*

*You stir us to take pleasure in praising you,*
*because you have made us for yourself,*
*and our heart is restless*
*until it rests in you.*

St. Augustine, *Confessions*

## **OPENING PRAYER**

Leader: + O God, come to my assistance,

All: O Lord, make haste to help me.

Leader: Glory to the Father, and to the Son, and to the Holy Spirit,

All: As it was in the beginning, is now, and will be for ever. Amen.

## **PSALM 63:1-8**

Leader: Each day I look to you, O God.

*Side 1 (Leader's Side)*
O God, you are my God, I seek you,
my soul thirsts for you;
my flesh faints for you,
as in a dry and weary land
where there is no water.

*Side 2*
So I look upon you in the sanctuary,
beholding your power and glory.
Because your steadfast love
is better than life,
my lips will praise you.

1

So I will bless you as long as I live;
I will lift up my hands
and call on your name.
My soul is satisfied as with a rich feast,
and my mouth praises you with joyful lips,

> 2
> When I think of you on my bed,
> and meditate on you
> in the watches of the night;
> for you have been my help,
>
> 1
> And in the shadow of your wings
> I sing for joy.
> My soul clings to you;
> your right hand upholds me.
>
>> 2
>> Glory to the Father, and to the Son,
>> and to the Holy Spirit,
>>
>> 1
>> As it was in the beginning, is now,
>> and will be for ever. Amen.
>
> All
> Each day I look to you, O God.

## FIRST READING

Ephesians 4:30–5:2

Reader: A reading from the letter to the Ephesians.

And do not grieve the Holy Spirit of God, with which you were marked with a seal for the day of redemption. Put away from you all bitterness and wrath and anger and wrangling and slander, together with all malice, and be kind to one another, tender-hearted, forgiving one another, as God in Christ has forgiven you. Therefore be imitators of God, as beloved children, and live in love, as Christ loved us and gave himself up for us, a fragrant offering and sacrifice to God.

Reader:     The word of the Lord.
All:        Thanks be to God.

## SONG OF SONGS 3:1-5

Leader:   Do not arouse, do not stir up love
          before its own time!

1
Upon my bed at night
I sought him, but found him not;
I called him, but he gave no answer.
2
"I will rise now and go about the city,
in the streets and in the squares;
I will seek him whom my soul loves."
I sought him, but found him not.
1
The sentinels found me,
as they went about in the city.
"Have you seen him whom my soul loves?"
2
Scarcely had I passed them,
when I found him whom my soul loves.
I held him, and would not let him go
until I brought him into my mother's house,
and into the chamber
of her that conceived me.
1
I adjure you, O daughters of Jerusalem,
by the gazelles or the wild does:
do not stir up or awaken love
until it is ready.
2
    Glory to the Father, and to the Son,
    and to the Holy Spirit,

1
As it was in the beginning, is now,
and will be for ever.  Amen.
All
Do not arouse, do not stir up love before
its own time.

## SECOND READING   1 Corinthians 7:7-8

Reader:   A reading from the first letter of
          Paul to the Corinthians.

I wish that all were as I myself am.  But
each has a particular gift from God, one
having one kind and another a different
kind.  To the unmarried and the widows
I say that it is well for them to remain
unmarried as I am.  But if they are not
practicing self-control, they should marry.
For it is better to marry than to be aflame
with passion.

Reader:     The word of the Lord.
All:        Thanks be to God.

## PSALM 117

Leader:   The Lord remains faithful to his
          promise for ever.

1
Praise the Lord, all you nations!
Extol him, all you peoples.

2
For great is his steadfast love toward us,
and the faithfulness of the Lord
endures forever.  Praise the Lord!

>     1
>     Glory to the Father, and to the Son,
>     and to the Holy Spirit,
>     2
>     As it was in the beginning, is now,
>     and will be for ever. Amen.

*All*

The Lord remains faithful to his promise for ever.

## THIRD READING        John 15:12-17

Reader:   A reading from the gospel of John.

This is my commandment, that you love one another as I have loved you. No one has greater love than this, to lay down one's life for one's friends. You are my friends if you do what I command you. I do not call you servants any longer, because the servant does not know what the master is doing; but I have called you friends, because I have made known to you everything that I have heard from my Father. You did not choose me but I chose you. And I appointed you to go and bear fruit, fruit that will last, so that the Father will give you whatever you ask him in my name. I am giving you these commands so that you may love one another.

Reader:    The gospel of the Lord.
All:       Praise to you, Lord Jesus Christ.

*Pause for silence.*

## JULY

# FREEDOM OF RELIGION

the american experiment

### Eternal, Invisible, God Only Wise

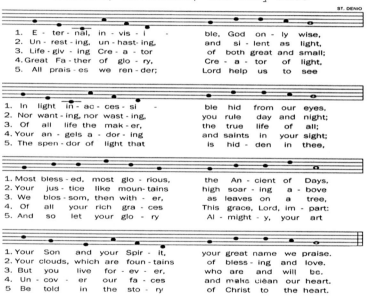

ST. DENIO

1. E-ter-nal, in-vis-i-ble, God on-ly wise,
   In light in-ac-ces-si-ble hid from our eyes,
   Most bless-ed, most glo-rious, the An-cient of Days,
   Your Son and your Spir-it, your great name we praise.
2. Un-rest-ing, un-hast-ing, and si-lent as light,
   Nor want-ing, nor wast-ing, you rule day and night;
   Your jus-tice like moun-tains high soar-ing a-bove
   Your clouds, which are foun-tains of bless-ing and love.
3. Life-giv-ing Cre-a-tor of both great and small;
   Of all life the mak-er, the true life of all;
   We blos-som, then with-er, as leaves on a tree,
   But you live for-ev-er, who are and will be.
4. Great Fa-ther of glo-ry, Cre-a-tor of light,
   Your an-gels a-dor-ing and saints in your sight;
   Of all your rich gra-ces This grace, Lord, im-part:
   Un-cov-er our fa-ces and make clean our heart.
5. All prais-es we ren-der; Lord help us to see
   The spen-dor of light that is hid-den in thee,
   And so let your glo-ry Al-might-y, your art
   Be told in the sto-ry of Christ to the heart.

Text: based on 1 Timothy 1:17; *Immortal Invisible God Only Wise*, Walter C. Smith, 1824-1908, *Hymns of Christ and the Christian Life* 1876, altered

Music: 11 11 11 11, ST. DENIO, Welsh Melody, John Roberts, 1822-1877, *Canaidau y Cyssegr*, 1839

*God has determined, unless I interfere
with God's plan, that I should reach that which
will be my greatest happiness. God looks on me
individually. God calls me by my name.
God knows what I can do, what I can best be,
what is my greatest happiness,
and God means to give it to me.*

John Henry Newman

## Opening Prayer

Leader: + O God, come to my assistance,

All: O Lord, make haste to help me.

Leader: Glory to the Father, and to the Son,
and to the Holy Spirit,

All: As it was in the beginning, is now,
and will be for ever. Amen.

## Psalm 67

Leader: Let the peoples praise you, O God,
let all the peoples praise you.

*Side 1 (Leader's Side)*
May God be gracious to us and bless us
and make his face to shine upon us,
that your way may be known upon earth,
your saving power among all nations.

*Side 2*
Let the peoples praise you, O God;
let all the peoples praise you.

1

Let the nations be glad and sing for joy,
for you judge the peoples with equity
and guide the nations upon earth.

2

Let the peoples praise you, O God;
let all the peoples praise you.

1

The earth has yielded its increase;
God, our God, has blessed us.
May God continue to bless us;
let all the ends of the earth revere him.

2
Glory to the Father, and to the Son,
and to the Holy Spirit,
1
As it was in the beginning, is now,
and will be for ever. Amen.

All
Let the peoples praise you, O God,
let all the peoples praise you.


## First Reading

James 3:13-18

Reader:  A reading from the letter of James.

Who is wise and understanding among you?
Show by your good life that your works
are done with gentleness born of wisdom.
But if you have bitter envy and selfish
ambition in your hearts, do not be boastful
and false to the truth. Such wisdom does
not come down from above, but is earthly,
unspiritual, devilish. For where there is
envy and selfish ambition, there will also
be disorder and wickedness of every kind.
But the wisdom from above is pure, then
peaceable, gentle, willing to yield, full
of mercy and good fruits, without a trace
of partiality or hypocrisy. And a harvest
of righteousness is sown in peace for
those who make peace.

Reader:     The word of the Lord.
All:        Thanks be to God.

## Psalm 40

Leader: Doing my Father's will is the food
that sustains me.

1
I waited patiently for the Lord;
he inclined to me and heard my cry.
2
He drew me up from the desolate pit,
out of the miry bog,
and set my feet upon a rock,
making my steps secure.
1
He put a new song in my mouth,
a song of praise to our God.
Many will see and fear,
and put their trust in the Lord.
2
Happy are those
who make the Lord their trust,
who do not turn to the proud,
to those who go astray after false gods.
1
You have multiplied, O Lord my God,
your wondrous deeds
and your thoughts toward us;
none can compare with you.
Were I to proclaim and tell of them,
they would be more than can be counted.
2
Sacrifice and offering you do not desire,
but you have given me an open ear.
Burnt offering and sin offering
you have not required.

# FREEDOM OF RELIGION

### 1
Then I said, "Here I am;
in the scroll of the book
it is written of me.
I delight to do your will, O my God;
your law is within my heart."

### 2
I have told the glad news of deliverance
in the great congregation;
see, I have not restrained my lips,
as you know, O Lord.

### 1
I have not hidden your saving help
within my heart,
I have spoken of your faithfulness
and your salvation;
I have not concealed your steadfast love
and your faithfulness
from the great congregation.

### 2
Do not, O Lord, withhold your mercy from me;
let your steadfast love
and your faithfulness keep me safe forever.

### 1
For evils have encompassed me
without number;
my iniquities have overtaken me,
until I cannot see;
they are more than the hairs of my head,
and my heart fails me.

### 2
Be pleased, O Lord, to deliver me;
O Lord, make haste to help me…

### 1
May all who seek you
rejoice and be glad in you;
may those who love your salvation
say continually, "Great is the Lord!"

> **2**
> As for me, I am poor and needy,
> but the Lord takes thought for me.
> You are my help and my deliverer;
> do not delay, O my God.

>> **1**
>> Glory to the Father, and to the Son,
>> and to the Holy Spirit,
>>
>> **2**
>> As it was in the beginning, is now,
>> and will be for ever. Amen.

**All**
Doing my Father's will is the food that sustains me.

## PSALM 84

Leader: One day within your courts is better than a thousand elsewhere.

**1**
How lovely is your dwelling place,
O Lord of hosts!

**2**
My soul longs, indeed it faints
for the courts of the Lord;
my heart and my flesh sing for joy
to the living God.

**1**
Even the sparrow finds a home,
and her swallow a nest for herself,
where she may lay her young,
at your altars, O Lord of hosts,
my King and my God.

2
Happy are those who live in your house,
ever singing your praise.
Happy are those whose strength is in you,
in whose heart are the highways to Zion.
1
As they go through the valley of Baca
they make it a place of springs;
the early rain also covers it with pools.
They go from strength to strength;
the God of gods will be seen in Zion.
2
O Lord God of hosts, hear my prayer;
give ear, O God of Jacob!
Behold our shield, O God;
look on the face of your anointed.
1
For a day in your courts is better
than a thousand elsewhere.
I would rather be a doorkeeper
in the house of my God
than live in the tents of wickedness.
2
For the Lord God is a sun and shield;
he bestows favor and honor.
No good thing does the Lord withhold
from those who walk uprightly.
1
O Lord of hosts,
happy is everyone who trusts in you.

> 2
> Glory to the Father, and to the Son,
> and to the Holy Spirit,
> 1
> As it was in the beginning, is now,
> and will be for ever.  Amen.

> All

One day within your courts is better than
a thousand elsewhere.

## SECOND READING Luke 4:16-22

Reader: A reading from the gospel of Luke.

When he came to Nazareth, where he had
been brought up, he went to the synagogue
on the sabbath day, as was his custom.
He stood up to read, and the scroll of
the prophet Isaiah was given to him.
He unrolled the scroll and found the place
where it was written:
"The Spirit of the Lord is upon me,
 because he has anointed me
 to bring good news to the poor.
 He has sent me to proclaim
 release to the captives
 and recovery of sight to the blind,
 to let the oppressed go free,
 to proclaim the year of the Lord's favor."
And he rolled up the scroll, gave it back
to the attendant, and sat down. The eyes
of all in the synagogue were fixed on him.
Then he began to say to them,
 "Today this scripture has been fulfilled
  in your hearing."
All spoke well of him and were amazed at
the gracious words that came from his mouth.
They said, "Is not this Joseph's son?"

Reader: The gospel of the Lord.
All: Praise to you, Lord Jesus Christ.

*Pause for silence.*

## August

# FOOD, CLOTHING AND SHELTER

### widows, aliens and orphans

### Holy Joseph, You Saluting

PLEADING SAVIOR

1. Ho - ly_ Jo- seph_, you sa - lut - ing  Here we_  meet, with_ hearts sin - cere;
2. You who_ faith - ful_ - ly at - tend - ed  Him whom_ heav'n and_ earth a - dore;
3. May our_ trust- ing_ voic - es lift - ing  Move you_ for our_ souls to pray;
4. Through this_ life, give_ watch a - round us! Thank our_ Lord for_ ev - 'ry breath,

1. Bless - ed_ Jo- seph_ all u - nite and  Call on_ you to_ hear our prayer.
2. Who with_ ten - der_ care de - fend - ed  Ma - ry_, Vir - gin_ ev - er pure.
3. May your_ smile of_ peace de - scend- ing,  Ben - e_ - dic -tions on us lay.
4. And, when_ part - ing_ fear sur - rounds us,  Guide us_ e - ven_ through our death.

1-4. Hap - py_ saint, in heav - en a - dor - ing  Je - sus_, Sav - ior of the_ race,

1-4. Hear your_ chil - dren_, fos - ter chil - dren,  May we_ find with_ you our place.

Text: anonymous, altered significantly

Music: 87 87 D, PLEADING SAVIOR, Joshua Leavitt, *Christian Lyre*, 1830

Traditional Melody for: *Sing of Mary, Pure and Lowly*

*When we attend to the needs of those in want,
we give them what is theirs, not ours.
More than performing works of mercy,
we are paying a debt of justice.*

St. Gregory the Great

## **OPENING PRAYER**

Leader:  + O God, come to my assistance,

All:  O Lord, make haste to help me.

Leader:  Glory to the Father, and to the Son, and to the Holy Spirit,

All:  As it was in the beginning, is now, and will be for ever. Amen.

## **ISAIAH 58:6-11**

Leader:  The Lord will guide you completely.

*Side 1 (Leader's Side)*
Is not this the fast that I choose:
to loose the bonds of injustice,
to undo the thongs of the yoke,
to let the oppressed go free,
and to break every yoke?

*Side 2*
Is it not
to share your bread with the hungry,
and bring the homeless poor
into your house;
when you see the naked, to cover them,
and not to hide yourself from your own kin?

1
Then your light shall break forth
like the dawn,
and your healing shall spring up quickly;
your vindicator shall go before you,
the glory of the Lord
shall be your rear guard.

2

Then you shall call,
and the Lord will answer;
you shall cry for help,
and he will say, Here I am.
If you remove the yoke from among you,
the pointing of the finger,
the speaking of evil,

1

If you offer your food to the hungry
and satisfy the needs of the afflicted,
then your light shall rise in the darkness
and your gloom be like the noonday.

2

The Lord will guide you continually,
and satisfy your needs in parched places,
and make your bones strong;

1

And you shall be like a watered garden,
like a spring of water,
whose waters never fail.

2

Your ancient ruins shall be rebuilt;
you shall raise up the foundations
of many generations;
you shall be called
the repairer of the breach,
the restorer of streets to live in.

1

If you refrain from trampling the sabbath,
from pursuing your own interests
on my holy day;
if you call the sabbath a delight
and the holy day of the Lord honorable;
if you honor it, not going your own ways,
serving your own interests,
or pursuing your own affairs;

2
Then you shall take delight in the Lord,
and I will make you ride upon
the heights of the earth;
I will feed you
with the heritage of your ancestor Jacob,
for the mouth of the Lord has spoken.

1
> Glory to the Father, and to the Son,
> and to the Holy Spirit,
> 2
> As it was in the beginning, is now,
> and will be for ever.  Amen.

All
The Lord will guide you completely.


## FIRST READING

Deuteronomy 10:12-20a

Reader:   A reading from the book of
          Deuteronomy.

So now, O Israel, what does the Lord your
God require of you?  Only to fear the Lord
your God, to walk in all his ways, to love
him, to serve the Lord your God with all
your heart and with all your soul, and to
keep the commandments of the Lord your God
and his decrees that I am commanding you
today, for your own well-being.  Although
heaven and the heaven of heavens belong to
the Lord your God, the earth with all that
is in it, yet the Lord set his heart in
love on your ancestors alone and chose you,
their descendants after them, out of all
the peoples, as it is today.  Circumcise,
then, the foreskin of your heart, and do

not be stubborn any longer. For the Lord
your God is God of gods and Lord of lords,
the great God, mighty and awesome, who
is not partial and takes no bribe, who
executes justice for the orphan and the
widow, and who loves the strangers,
providing them food and clothing. You
shall also love the stranger, for you were
strangers in the land of Egypt. You shall
shall fear the Lord your God; him alone
you shall worship.

Reader:     The word of the Lord.
All:        Thanks be to God.


## PSALM 73

Leader: My joy is to remain with you, O God.

1

Truly God is good to the upright,
to those who are pure in heart.
But as for me, my feet had almost stumbled;
my steps had nearly slipped.

2

For I was envious of the arrogant;
I saw the prosperity of the wicked.
For they have no pain;
their bodies are sound and sleek.
They are not in trouble as others are;
they are not plagued like other people.

1

Therefore pride is their necklace;
violence covers them like a garment.
Their eyes swell out with fatness;
their hearts overflow with follies.

2
They scoff and speak with malice;
loftily they threaten oppression.
They set their mouths against heaven,
and their tongues range over the earth.

1
Therefore the people turn and praise them,
and find no fault in them.
And they say, "How can God know?
Is there knowledge in the Most High?"
Such are the wicked;
always at ease, they increase in riches.

2
All in vain I have kept my heart clean
and washed my hands in innocence.
For all day long I have been plagued,
and am punished every morning.

1
If I had said, "I will talk on in this way,"
I would have been untrue
to the circle of your children.

2
But when I thought how to understand this,
it seemed to me a wearisome task,
until I went into the sanctuary of God;
then I perceived their end.

1
Truly you set them in slippery places;
you make them fall to ruin.
How they are destroyed in a moment,
swept away utterly by terrors!
They are like a dream when one awakes;
on awaking you despise their phantoms.

2
When my soul was embittered,
when I was pricked in heart,
I was stupid and ignorant;
I was like a brute beast toward you.

FOOD, CLOTHING AND SHELTER 75

<sub>1</sub>
Nevertheless I am continually with you;
you hold my right hand.
You guide me with your counsel,
and afterward you will receive me with honor.

<sub>2</sub>
Whom have I in heaven but you?
And there is nothing on earth that I desire
other than you.
My flesh and my heart may fail,
but God is the strength of my heart
and my portion forever.

<sub>1</sub>
Indeed,
those who are far from you will perish;
you put an end
to those who are false to you.
But for me it is good to be near God;
I have made the Lord God my refuge,
to tell of all your works.

<sub>2</sub>
>Glory to the Father, and to the Son,
>and to the Holy Spirit,

<sub>1</sub>
>As it was in the beginning, is now,
>and will be for ever. Amen.

All
My joy is to remain with you, O God.

## SECOND READING

Job 31:16-28a

Reader:   A reading from the book of Job.

If I have withheld anything that the
poor desired, or have caused the eyes of
the widow to fail, or have eaten my morsel
alone, and the orphan has not eaten from it
—for from my youth I reared the orphan like

a father, and from my mother's womb I guided the widow - if I have seen anyone perish for lack of clothing, or a poor person without covering, whose loins have not blessed me, and who was not warmed with the fleece of my sheep; if I have raised my hand against the orphan, because I saw I had supporters at the gate; then let my shoulder blade fall from my shoulder, and let my arm be broken from its socket… If I have made gold my trust, or called fine gold my confidence; if I have rejoiced because my wealth was great, or because my hand had gotten much; if I have looked at the sun when it shone, or the moon moving in splendor, and my heart has been secretly enticed, and my mouth has kissed my hand; this also would be an iniquity…

Reader: The word of the Lord.
All: Thanks be to God.

## Psalm 96

Leader: Sing to the Lord and bless his name.

1
O sing to the Lord a new song;
sing to the Lord, all the earth.
Sing to the Lord, bless his name;

2
Tell of his salvation from day to day.
Declare his glory among the nations,
his marvelous works among all the peoples.

1
For great is the Lord,
and greatly to be praised;
he is to be revered above all gods.
For all the gods of the peoples are idols,

> 2

But the Lord made the heavens.
Honor and majesty are before him;
strength and beauty are in his sanctuary.

> 1

Ascribe to the Lord,
O families of the peoples,
ascribe to the Lord glory and strength.
Ascribe to the Lord the glory due his name;

> 2

Bring an offering, and come into his courts.
Worship the Lord in holy splendor;
tremble before him, all the earth.

> 1

Say among the nations, "The Lord is king!
The world is firmly established;
it shall never be moved.
He will judge the peoples with equity."

> 2

Let the heavens be glad,
and let the earth rejoice;
let the sea roar, and all that fills it;
let the field exult, and everything in it.

> 1

Then shall all the trees of the forest
sing for joy before the Lord;
for he is coming,
for he is coming to judge the earth.
He will judge the world with righteousness,
and the peoples with his truth.

> 2

> Glory to the Father, and to the Son,
> and to the Holy Spirit,

> 1

> As it was in the beginning, is now,
> and will be for ever.  Amen.

*All*

Sing to the Lord and bless his name.

## THIRD READING

Matthew 25:31-40

Reader: A reading from the gospel of Matthew.

"When the Son of Man comes in his glory, and all the angels with him, then he will sit on the throne of his glory. All the nations will be gathered before him, and he will separate people one from another as a shepherd separates the sheep from the goats, and he will put the sheep at his right hand and the goats at the left. Then the king will say to those at his right hand, 'Come, you that are blessed by my Father, inherit the kingdom prepared for you from the foundation of the world; for I was hungry and you gave me food, I was thirsty and you gave me something to drink, I was a stranger and you welcomed me, I was naked and you gave me clothing, I was sick and you took care of me, I was in prison and you visited me.' Then the righteous will answer him, Lord, when was it that we saw you hungry and gave you food, or thirsty and gave you something to drink? And when was it that we saw you sick or in prison and visited you?' And the king will answer them, Truly I tell you, just as you did it to one of the least of these who are members of my family, you did it to me'"

Reader: The gospel of the Lord.
All: Praise to you, Lord Jesus Christ.

*Pause for silence.*

## September

# EDUCATION

the right that can be the key

### Lord, Your Almighty Word

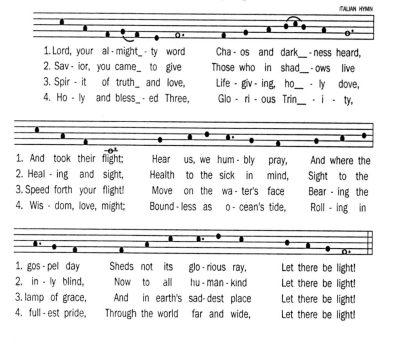

1. Lord, your al-might-ty word / Cha-os and dark—-ness heard, / And took their flight; / Hear us, we hum-bly pray, / And where the gos-pel day / Sheds not its glo-rious ray, / Let there be light!
2. Sav-ior, you came to give / Those who in shad—-ows live / Heal-ing and sight, / Health to the sick in mind, / Sight to the in-ly blind, / Now to all hu-man-kind / Let there be light!
3. Spir-it of truth and love, / Life-giv-ing, ho—-ly dove, / Speed forth your flight! / Move on the wa-ter's face / Bear-ing the lamp of grace, / And in earth's sad-dest place / Let there be light!
4. Ho-ly and bless—-ed Three, / Glo-ri-ous Trin—-i-ty, / Wis-dom, love, might; / Bound-less as o-cean's tide, / Roll-ing in full-est pride, / Through the world far and wide, / Let there be light!

Text: Based on Genesis 1:3, *Thou Whose Almighty Word*, 1813, John Marriott, 1780-1825, altered

Music: 664 6664, ITALIAN HYMN (MOSCOW), Felice de Giardini, 1716-1796, 1769

*Faith seeks understanding.*

St. Anselm

## **OPENING PRAYER**

Leader: + O God, come to my assistance,

All: O Lord, make haste to help me.

Leader: Glory to the Father, and to the Son,
and to the Holy Spirit,

All: As it was in the beginning, is now,
and will be for ever. Amen.

## **PSALM 71**

Leader: I have trusted in you, O Lord,
from my youth.

Side 1 (Leader's Side)
In you, O Lord, I take refuge;
let me never be put to shame.
In your righteousness
deliver me and rescue me;
incline your ear to me and save me.

Side 2
Be to me a rock of refuge,
a strong fortress, to save me,
for you are my rock and my fortress.
Rescue me, O my God,
from the hand of the wicked,
from the grasp of the unjust and cruel.

1

For you, O Lord, are my hope,
my trust, O Lord, from my youth.
Upon you I have leaned from my birth;
it was you who took me from my mother's womb.
My praise is continually of you.

# EDUCATION

2

I have been like a portent to many,
but you are my strong refuge.
My mouth is filled with your praise,
and with your glory all day long.

1

Do not cast me off in the time of old age;
do not forsake me when my strength is spent.
For my enemies speak concerning me,
and those who watch for my life
consult together.

2

They say, "Pursue and seize that person
whom God has forsaken,
for there is no one to deliver."
O God, do not be far from me;
O my God, make haste to help me!

1

Let my accusers be put to shame and consumed;
let those who seek to hurt me
be covered with scorn and disgrace.
But I will hope continually,
and will praise you yet more and more.
My mouth will tell of your righteous acts,
of your deeds of salvation all day long,
though their number is past my knowledge.

2

I will come praising
the mighty deeds of the Lord God,
I will praise your righteousness,
yours alone.
O God, from my youth you have taught me,
and I still proclaim your wondrous deeds.

1

So even to old age and gray hairs,
O God, do not forsake me,
until I proclaim your might
to all the generations to come.

2

Your power and your righteousness, O God,
reach the highest heavens.
You who have done great things,
O God, who is like you?

1

You who have made me see
many troubles and calamities
will revive me again;
from the depths of the earth
you will bring me up again.
You will increase my honor,
and comfort me once again.

2

I will also praise you with the harp
for your faithfulness, O my God;
I will sing praises to you with the lyre,
O Holy One of Israel.

1

My lips will shout for joy
when I sing praises to you;
my soul also, which you have rescued.
All day long my tongue will talk
of your righteous help…

2

>  Glory to the Father, and to the Son,
>  and to the Holy Spirit,

1

>  As it was in the beginning, is now,
>  and will be for ever.  Amen.

All

I have trusted in you, O Lord,
from my youth.

EDUCATION

## First Reading

1 Kings 3:11-14

Reader:   A reading from the 1st book of Kings.

It pleased the Lord that Solomon had asked
this. God said to him, "Because you have
asked this, and have not asked for yourself
long life or riches, or for the life of
your enemies, but have asked for yourself
understanding to discern what is right,
I now do according to your word. Indeed
I give you a wise and discerning mind;
no one like you has been before you and
no one like you shall arise after you.
I give you also what you have not asked,
both riches and honor all your life;
no other king shall compare with you.
If you walk in my ways, keeping my statutes
and my commandments, as your father David
walked, then I will lengthen your life."

Reader:      The word of the Lord.
All:         Thanks be to God.

## Wisdom 9:1-6,9-11

Leader:   Wisdom of God, be with me,
          always at work within me.

1

O God of my ancestors and Lord of mercy,
who have made all things by your word,
and by your wisdom have formëd humankind
to have dominion over
the creatures you have made,

2

And rule the world
in holiness and righteousness,
and pronounce judgment
in uprightness of soul,
give me wisdom that sits by your throne,
and do not reject me
from among your servants.

1

For I am your servant
the son of your servant girl,
a man who is weak and short-lived,
with little understanding
of judgment and laws;

2

Even one who is perfect among human beings
will be regarded as nothing
without the wisdom that comes from you.

1

With you is wisdom,
she who knows your works
and was present when you made the world;
she understands
what is pleasing in your sight
and what is right
according to your commandments.

2

Send her forth from the holy heavens,
and from the throne of your glory send her,
that she may labor at my side,
and that I may learn
what is pleasing to you.

1

For she knows and understands all things,
and she will guide me wisely in my actions
and guard me with her glory.

2
Glory to the Father, and to the Son,
and to the Holy Spirit,
1
As it was in the beginning, is now,
and will be for ever. Amen.

All
Wisdom of God, be with me, always at work within me.


## SECOND READING

Deuteronomy 6:20-24

Reader: A reading from the book of Deuteronomy.

When your children ask you in time to come, "What is the meaning of the decrees and statutes and the ordinances that the Lord our God has commanded you?" then you shall say to your children, "We were Pharoah's slaves in Egypt, but the Lord brought us out of Egypt with a mighty hand. The Lord displayed before our eyes great and awesome signs and wonders against Egypt, against Pharaoh and all his household. He brought us out from there in order to bring us in, to give us the land that he promised on oath to our ancestors. Then the Lord commanded us to observe these statutes, to fear the Lord our God, for our lasting good, so as to keep us alive, as is now the case.

Reader: The word of the Lord.
All: Thanks be to God.

## PSALM 104

Leader:  The Lord looked upon all creation
and saw that it was very good.

1

Bless the Lord, O my soul.
O Lord my God, you are very great.
You are clothed with honor and majesty,
wrapped in light as with a garment.

2

You stretch out the heavens like a tent,
you set the beams of your chambers
on the waters,
you make the clouds your chariot,
you ride on the wings of the wind,
you make the winds your messengers,
fire and flame your ministers.

1

You set the earth on its foundations,
so that it shall never be shaken.
You cover it with the deep
as with a garment;
the waters stood above the mountains.

2

At your rebuke they flee;
at the sound of your thunder
they take to flight.
They rose up to the mountains,
ran down to the valleys
to the place that you appointed for them.
You set a boundary that they may not pass,
so that they might not again cover the earth.

1

You make springs gush forth in the valleys;
they flow between the hills,
giving drink to every wild animal;
the wild asses quench their thirst.

2

By the streams the birds of the air
have their habitation;
they sing among the branches.
From your lofty abode
you water the mountains;
the earth is satisfied
with the fruit of your work.

1

You cause the grass to grow for the cattle,
and plants for people to use,
to bring forth food from the earth,
and wine to gladden the human heart,
oil to make the face shine,
and bread to strengthen the human heart.

2

The trees of the Lord
are watered abundantly,
the cedars of Lebanon that he planted.
In them the birds build their nests;
the stork has its home in the fir trees.
The high mountains are for the wild goats;
the rocks are a refuge for the coneys.

1

You have made the moon to mark the seasons;
the sun knows its time for setting.
You make darkness, and it is night,
when all the animals of the forest
come creeping out.
The young lions roar for their prey,
seeking their food from God.

2

When the sun rises, they withdraw
and lie down in their dens.
People go out to their work
and to their labor until the evening.

1
O Lord, how manifold are your works!
in wisdom you have made them all;
the earth is full of your creatures.
2
Yonder is the sea, great and wide,
creeping things innumerable are there,
living things both small and great.
There go the ships,
and Leviathan that you formed
to sport in it.
1
These all look to you
to give them their food in due season;
when you give it to them,
they gather it up;
when you open your hand,
they are filled with good things.
2
When you hide your face, they are dismayed;
when you take away their breath,
they die and return to their dust.
When you send forth your spirit,
they are created;
and you renew the face of the ground.
1
May the glory of the Lord endure forever;
may the Lord rejoice in his works –
who looks on the earth and it trembles,
who touches the mountains and they smoke.
2
I will sing to the Lord as long as I live;
I will sing praise to my God
while I have being.
May my meditation be pleasing to him,
for I rejoice in the Lord...

EDUCATION

1
Bless the Lord, O my soul.
Praise the Lord!
2
> Glory to the Father, and to the Son,
> and to the Holy Spirit,
1
> As it was in the beginning, is now,
> and will be for ever. Amen.

All
The Lord looked upon all creation,
and saw that it was very good.


## THIRD READING           Matthew 5:1-12

Reader: A reading from the gospel of Matthew.

When Jesus saw the crowds, he went up the
mountain; and after he sat down, his
disciples came to him. Then he began to
speak, and taught them, saying:
"Blessed are the poor in spirit,
   for theirs is the kingdom of heaven.
 Blessed are those who mourn,
   for they will be comforted.
 Blessed are the meek,
   for they will inherit the earth.
 Blessed are those who hunger and thirst
     for righteousness,
   for they will be filled.
 Blessed are the merciful,
   for they will receive mercy.
 Blessed are the pure in heart,
   for they will see God.
 Blessed are the peacemakers,
   for they will be called children of God.

> Blessed are those who are persecuted for
>    righteousness' sake,
>   for theirs is the kingdom of heaven.
> Blessed are you, when people revile you
>   and persecute you and utter all kinds of
>   evil against you falsely on my account.
>   Rejoice and be glad, for your reward
>   is great in heaven, for in the same way
>   they persecuted the prophets who were
>   before you."

Reader: The gospel of the Lord.
All: Praise to you, Lord Jesus Christ.

*Pause for silence.*

**In a word, we can say that the cultural change**
**which we are calling for demands from everyone**
**the courage to adopt a new life-style**
**consisting in making practical choices**
**-at the personal, family, social and international level-**
**on the basis of a correct scale of values:**
**the primacy of being over having,**
**of the person over things.**
**This renewed life-style involves a passing**
**from indifference to concern for others,**
**from rejection to acceptance of them.**
**Other people are not rivals**
**from whom we must defend ourselves,**
**but brothers and sisters to be supported.**
**They are to be loved for their own sakes,**
**and they enrich us by their presence.**

The Gospel of Life (*Evangelium Vitae*), Pope John Paul II, 1995, #98

## OCTOBER

# NATURAL DYING

## resisting suicide assistance

Jerusalem, My Happy Home

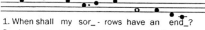

LAND OF REST

1. Je - ru - sa - lem_, my hap - py home_, When shall I come_ to thee?
2. O hap - py har_ - bor of the saints_! O sweet and pleas_- ant soil!
3. The saints are crowned_ with glo - ry great_; They see God face_ to face;
4. Your gar - dens and_ your gal - lant walks Con - tin - ual - ly_ are green:
5. There trees for - ev_ - er - more bear fruit_, And ev - er - more_ do spring;
6. King Da - vid stands_, his harp in hand_ As lead - er of_ the choir:
7. Our La - dy sings_ Mag - ni - fi - cat_ With tune sur - pas_ - sing sweet,
8. And Mag - da - len_ has left her grief_, With cheer- ful joy_ does sing
9. Je - ru - sa - lem_, Je - ru - sa - lem_, God grant that I_ may see

1. When shall my sor_ - rows have an end_? Your joys when shall_ I see?
2. In you no sor_ - rows may be found_, No grief, no wor - ry or toil.
3. They tri - umph still_, they still re - joice_ Most hap - py is_ their case.
4. There grow such sweet_ and pleas- ant flow'rs_ As no - where else_ are seen.
5. There ev - er - more_ the ang - els are_, And ev - er - more_ do sing.
6. Ten thous- and times_ that we be blessed_, That we this mu_ - sic hear.
7. And all the vir_ - gins bear their part_, While sit - ting at_ her feet.
8. And bless - ed saints_, their har - mo - ny_ To ev - 'ry room_ they bring.
9. Your end - less joy_, and of the same_ Par - ta - ker al_ - ways be.

Text: F.B.P., London, around 1583, altered
Music: C.M. 86 86, LAND OF REST, traditional American Melody

*Praised be my Lord for our sister,*
*the death of the body,*
*from which no one escapes.*

St. Francis of Assisi, *Canticle of the Sun*

*...I do not know which I prefer.*
*I am hard pressed between the two...*

St. Paul, *Philippians 1:22b-23a*

## Opening Prayer

Leader: + O God, come to my assistance,

All: O Lord, make haste to help me.

Leader: Glory to the Father, and to the Son,
and to the Holy Spirit,

All: As it was in the beginning, is now,
and will be for ever. Amen.

## Psalm 143:1-11

Leader: Do not hide your face from me;
in you I put my trust.

*Side 1 (Leader's Side)*

Hear my prayer, O Lord;
give ear to my supplications
in your faithfulness;
answer me in your righteousness.
Do not enter into judgment with your servant,
for no one living is righteous before you.

*Side 2*

For the enemy has pursued me,
crushing my life to the ground,
making me sit in darkness
like those long dead.
Therefore my spirit faints within me;
my heart within me is appalled.

1

I remember the days of old,
I think about all your deeds,
I meditate on the works of your hands,
I stretch out my hands to you;
my soul thirsts for you like a parched land.

2
Answer me quickly, O Lord;
my spirit fails.
Do not hide your face from me,
or I shall be like those
who go down to the Pit.
1
Let me hear
of your steadfast love in the morning,
for in you I put my trust.
Teach me the way I should go,
for to you I lift up my soul.
2
Save me, O Lord, from my enemies;
I have fled to you for refuge.
Teach me to do your will,
for you are my God.
Let your good spirit lead me
on a level path.
1
For your name's sake, O Lord,
preserve my life.
In your righteousness
bring me out of trouble.

> 2
> Glory to the Father, and to the Son,
> and to the Holy Spirit,
> 1
> As it was in the beginning, is now,
> and will be for ever. Amen.

All
Do not hide your face from me,
in you I put my trust.

## **First Reading**  Romans 8:18-28

Reader: A reading from the letter of Paul to the Romans.

I consider that the sufferings of this present time are not worth comparing with the glory about to be revealed to us. For the creation waits with eager longing for the revealing of the children of God; for the creation was subjected to futility, but not of its own will but by the will of the one who subjected it, in hope that the creation itself will be set free from its bondage to decay and will obtain the freedom of the glory of the children of God. We know that the whole creation has been groaning in labor pains until now; and not only the creation, but we ourselves, who have the first fruits of the Spirit, groan inwardly while we wait for adoption, the redemption of our bodies. For in hope we were saved. Now hope that is seen is not hope. For who hopes for what is seen? But if we hope for what we do not see, we wait for it with patience. Likewise the Spirit helps us in our weakness; for we do not know how to pray as we ought, but that very Spirit intercedes with sighs too deep for words. And God, who searches the heart, knows what is the mind of the Spirit, because the Spirit intercedes for the saints according to the will of God. We know that all things work together for good for those who love God, who are called according to his purpose.

NATURAL DYING

Reader: The word of the Lord.
All: Thanks be to God.

## PSALM 91

Leader: Night holds no terrors for me
sleeping under God's wings.

1

You who live
in the shelter of the Most High,
who abide in the shadow of the Almighty,
will say to the Lord,
"My refuge and my fortress;
my God in whom I trust."

2

For he will deliver you
from the snare of the fowler
and from the deadly pestilence;
he will cover you with his pinions,
and under his wings you will find refuge;
his faithfulness is a shield and buckler.

1

You will not fear the terror of the night,
or the arrow that flies by day,
or the pestilence that stalks in darkness,
or the destruction that wastes at noonday.

2

A thousand may fall at your side,
ten thousand at your right hand,
but it will not come near you.
You will only look with your eyes
and see the punishment of the wicked.

1
Because you have made the Lord your refuge,
the Most High your dwelling place,
no evil shall befall you,
no scourge come near your tent.
2
For he will command his angels
concerning you,
to guard you in all your ways.
On their hands they shall bear you up,
so that you will not dash your foot
against a stone.

1
You will tread on the lion and the adder,
the young lion and the serpent
you will trample underfoot.
2
Those who love me, I will deliver;
I will protect those who know my name.
When they call to me, I will answer them;
I will be with them in trouble,
I will rescue them and honor them.

1
With long life I will satisfy them,
and show them my salvation.
2
> Glory to the Father, and to the Son,
> and to the Holy Spirit,
1
> As it was in the beginning, is now,
> and will be for ever.  Amen.

All

Night holds no terrors for me
sleeping under God's wings.

## Second Reading

James 5:13-16

Reader:   A reading from the letter of James.

Are any among you suffering? They should pray. Are any cheerful? They should sing songs of praise. Are any among you sick? They should call for the elders of the church and have them pray over them, anointing them with oil in the name of the Lord. The prayer of faith will save the sick, and the Lord will raise them up; and anyone who has committed sins will be forgiven. Therefore confess your sins to one another, so that you may be healed. The prayer of the righteous is powerful and effective.

Reader:      The word of the Lord.
All:         Thanks be to God.

## Psalm 86

Leader:   O Lord, our God, unwearied is
          your love for us.

1
Incline your ear, O Lord, and answer me,
for I am poor and needy.
Preserve my life, for I am devoted to you;
save your servant who trusts in you.

2
You are my God; be gracious to me, O Lord,
for to you do I cry all day long.
Gladden the soul of your servant,
for to you, O Lord, I lift up my soul.

### 1

For you, O Lord, are good and forgiving,
abounding in steadfast love
to all who call on you.
Give ear, O Lord, to my prayer;
listen to my cry of supplication.

### 2

In the day of my trouble I call on you,
for you will answer me.
There is none like you
among the gods, O Lord,
nor are there any works like yours.

### 1

All the nations you have made shall come
and bow down before you, O Lord,
and shall glorify your name.
For you are great and do wonderful things;
you alone are God.

### 2

Teach me your way, O Lord,
that I may walk in your truth;
give me an undivided heart
to revere your name.

### 1

I give thanks to you, O Lord my God,
with my whole heart,
and I will glorify your name forever.
For great is your steadfast love toward me;
you have delivered my soul
from the depths of Sheol.

### 2

O God, the insolent rise up against me;
a band of ruffians seeks my life,
and they do not set you before them.

NATURAL DYING

1
But you, O Lord,
are a God merciful and gracious,
slow to anger and abounding
in steadfast love and faithfulness.

2
Turn to me and be gracious to me;
give your strength to your servant;
save the child of your serving girl.

1
Show me a sign of your favor,
so that those who hate me may see it
and be put to shame,
because you, Lord,
have helped me and comforted me.

2
>   Glory to the Father, and to the Son,
>   and to the Holy Spirit,

1
>   As it was in the beginning, is now,
>   and will be for ever. Amen.

All
O Lord, our God, unwearied is your love
for us.


## THIRD READING

Luke 10:25-37

Reader: A reading from the gospel of Luke.

Just then a lawyer stood up to test Jesus. "Teacher," he said, "what must I do to inherit eternal life?" He said to him, "What is written in the law? What do you read there?" He answered, "You shall love the Lord your God with all your heart, and with all your soul, and with all your strength, and with all your mind; and your neighbor as yourself." And he said to him, "You have given the right answer; do this, and you will live." But wanting to justify himself, he asked Jesus, "And who is my neighbor?" Jesus replied, "A man was going down from Jerusalem to Jericho, and fell into the hands of robbers, who stripped him, beat him, and went away, leaving him half dead. Now by chance a priest was going down that road; and when he saw him, he passed by on the other side. So likewise a Levite, when he came to the place and saw him, passed by on the other side. But a Samaritan while traveling came near to him; and when he saw him, he was moved with pity. He went to him and bandaged his wounds, having poured oil and wine on them. Then he put him on his own animal, brought him to an inn, and took care of him. The next day he took out two denarii, gave them to the innkeeper, and said, 'Take care of him; and when I come back, I will repay you whatever more you spend.' Which of these three, do you think, was a neighbor to the man who fell into the hands of the robbers?" He said, "The one who showed him mercy." Jesus said to him, "Go and do likewise."

Reader: The gospel of the Lord.
All: Praise to you, Lord Jesus Christ.

*Pause for silence.*

# November

# WORLD PEACE

peoples at war

## Comfort, Comfort, O My People

GENEVA 42

1. Com-fort, com-fort you my peo-ple,   Speak of peace, thus says our God;
2. For the her-ald's voice is cry-ing   In the des-ert far and near,
3. Yes, all sins our God will par-don,   Blot-ting each con-fessed mis-deed;
4. Make now straight what long was crook-ed,   Make the rough-er plac-es plain:

1. Com-fort those who sit in dark-ness,   Mourn-ing un-der sor-row's load;
2. Call-ing peo-ple to re-pent-ance   Since the king-dom now is here.
3. All that well de-served his ang-er   God will no more see nor heed.
4. Let our hearts be true and hum-ble,   As be-fits the ho-ly reign.

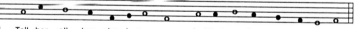

1. Speak un-to Jer-u-sa-lem   Of the peace that waits for them;
2. Now that warn-ing cry o-bey!   Now pre-pare for God a way!
3. We have suf-fered ma-ny days,   Now our grief has passed a-way;
4. For the glo-ry of the Lord   O-ver earth is shed a-broad.

1. Tell her all her sins I cov-er,   And that war-fare now is o-ver.
2. Let the val-leys rise to meet him,   And the hills bow down to greet him.
3. God will change our hea-vy sad-ness   In-to ev-er spring-ing glad-ness.
4. Hu-man be-ings, see the to-ken   That his word is nev-er bro-ken.

Text: based on Isaiah 40:1-8 for the Feast of John the Baptist, Johann G. Olearius, 1611-1684; translated by Catherine Winkworth, 1827-1878, altered

Music: 87 87 77 88, GENEVA 42, Claude Goudimel, 1514-1572, *Geneva Psalter*, 1551, altered at the end

*No peace without justice;
no justice without forgiveness.*

Pope John Paul II, response to September 11

## OPENING PRAYER

Leader: + O God, come to my assistance,

All: O Lord, make haste to help me.

Leader: Glory to the Father, and to the Son,
and to the Holy Spirit,

All: As it was in the beginning, is now,
and will be for ever. Amen.

## PSALM 24

Leader: Open wide the doors and gates;
Lift high the ancient portals.

Side 1 (Leader's Side)
The earth is the Lord's
and all that is in it,
the world, and those who live in it;
for he has founded it on the seas,
and established it on the rivers.

Side 2
Who shall ascend the hill of the Lord?
And who shall stand in his holy place?
Those who have clean hands and pure hearts,
who do not lift up their souls
to what is false,
and do not swear deceitfully.

1
They will receive blessing from the Lord,
and vindication from
the God of their salvation.
Such is the company of those who seek him,
who seek the face of the God of Jacob.

WORLD PEACE

2
Lift up your heads, O gates!
and be lifted up, O ancient doors!
that the King of glory may come in.
Who is the King of glory?
The Lord, strong and mighty,
the Lord, mighty in battle.

1
Lift up your heads, O gates!
and be lifted up, O ancient doors!
that the King of glory may come in.
Who is the King of glory?
The Lord of hosts, he is the King of glory.

2
> Glory to the Father, and to the Son,
> and to the Holy Spirit,

1
> As it was in the beginning, is now,
> and will be for ever. Amen.

All
Open wide the doors and gates;
lift high the ancient portals.


## FIRST READING

Isaiah 2:1-5

Reader:   A reading from the book of the
          prophet Isaiah.

The word that Isaiah son of Amoz saw
concerning Judah and Jerusalem.
In days to come
  the mountain of the Lord's house
shall be established as the highest of
     mountains,
  and shall be raised above the hills;

all nations shall stream to it.
  Many peoples shall come and say,
"Come, let us go up
  to the mountain of the Lord,
  to the house of the God of Jacob;
that he may teach us his ways
  and that we may walk in his paths."
For out of Zion shall go forth instruction,
  and the word of the Lord from Jerusalem.
He shall judge between the nations,
  and shall arbitrate for many peoples;
they shall beat their swords
    into plowshares,
  and their spears into pruning hooks;
nation shall not lift up sword
      against nation,
  neither shall they learn war any more.
O house of Jacob, come,
  let us walk in the light of the Lord!

Reader:    The word of the Lord.
All:       Thanks be to God.

### ISAIAH 11:1-10

Leader:   The earth will be full of the
          knowledge of the Lord.

1

A shoot shall come out
from the stump of Jesse,
and a branch shall grow out of his roots.
The spirit of the Lord shall rest on him,
the spirit of wisdom and understanding,
the spirit of counsel and might,
the spirit of knowledge
and the fear of the Lord.

# WORLD PEACE

2

His delight shall be in the fear of the Lord.
He shall not judge by what his eyes see,
or decide by what his ears hear;
but with righteousness
he shall judge the poor,
and decide with equity
for the meek of the earth;

1

He shall strike the earth
with the rod of his mouth,
and with the breath of his lips
he shall kill the wicked.
Righteousness shall be
the belt around his waist,
and faithfulness the belt around his loins.

2

The wolf shall live with the lamb,
the leopard shall lie down with the kid,
the calf and the lion
and the fatling together,
and a little child shall lead them.

1

The cow and the bear shall graze,
their young shall lie down together;
and the lion shall eat straw like the ox.

2

The nursing child shall play
over the hole of the asp,
and the weaned child shall put its hand
on the adder's den.

1

They will not hurt or destroy
on all my holy mountain;
for the earth will be full
of the knowledge of the Lord
as the waters cover the sea.

On that day the root of Jesse
shall stand as a signal to the peoples;
the nations shall inquire of him,
and his dwelling shall be glorious.

> Glory to the Father, and to the Son,
> and to the Holy Spirit,
>
> As it was in the beginning, is now,
> and will be for ever. Amen.

All
The earth will be full of the knowledge of the Lord.

## PSALM 82

Leader: There is but one lawgiver and judge;
who are you to judge your neighbor?

God has taken his place
in the divine council;
in the midst of the gods he holds judgment.

"How long will you judge unjustly
and show partiality to the wicked?
Give justice to the weak and the orphan;
maintain the right
of the lowly and the destitute.
Rescue the weak and the needy;
deliver them from the hand of the wicked."

WORLD PEACE

1
They have neither knowledge
nor understanding,
they walk around in darkness;
all the foundations of the earth are shaken.

2
I say, "You are gods,
children of the Most High, all of you;
nevertheless, you shall die like mortals,
and fall like any prince."

1
Rise up, O God, judge of the earth;
for all the nations belong to you!

2
> Glory to the Father, and to the Son,
> and to the Holy Spirit,

1
> As it was in the beginning, is now,
> and will be for ever. Amen.

All
There is but one lawgiver and judge;
who are you to judge your neighbor?

## SECOND READING

Deuteronomy 30:15-19

Reader: A reading from the book of Deuteronomy.

See, I have set before you today life and prosperity, death and adversity. If you obey the commandments of the Lord your God that I am commanding you today, by loving the Lord your God, walking in his ways, and observing his commandments, decrees, and ordinances, then you shall live and become numerous, and the Lord your God will bless

you in the land that you are entering
to possess.  But if your heart turns away
and you do not hear, but are led astray to
bow down to other gods and serve them, I
declare to you today that you shall perish;
you shall not live long in the land that
you are crossing the Jordan to enter and
possess.  I call heaven and earth to
witness against you today that I have
set before you life and death, blessings
and curses.  Choose life so that you
and your descendants may live.

Reader:     The word of the Lord.
All:        Thanks be to God.


## Psalm 122

Leader:   Pray for the peace of Jerusalem.

1

I was glad when they said to me,
"Let us go to the house of the Lord!"
Our feet are standing
within your gates, O Jerusalem.

2

Jerusalem - built as a city
that is bound firmly together.
To it the tribes go up,
the tribes of the Lord,

1

As was decreed for Israel,
to give thanks to the name of the Lord.
For there the thrones for judgment
were set up,
the thrones of the house of David.

                      2  
Pray for the peace of Jerusalem:  
"May they prosper who love you.  
Peace be within your walls,  
and security within your towers."  
                      1  
For the sake of my relatives and friends  
I will say, "Peace be within you."  
For the sake of the house  
of the Lord our God,  
I will seek your good.

                      2  
    Glory to the Father, and to the Son,  
    and to the Holy Spirit,  
                  1  
    As it was in the beginning, is now,  
    and will be for ever.  Amen.  
                  All  
Pray for the peace of Jerusalem.


## THIRD READING

Mark 2:1-12

Reader:   A reading from the gospel of Mark.

When he returned to Capernaum after some days, it was reported that he was at home. So many gathered around that there was no longer room for them, not even in front of the door; and he was speaking the word to them.  Then some people came, bringing him a paralyzed man, carried by four of them. And when they could not bring him to Jesus because of the crowd, they removed the roof above him; and after having dug through it, they let down the mat on which the paralytic lay.  When Jesus saw their faith, he said to the paralytic, "Son, your sins are forgiven." Now some of the scribes were sitting there, questioning in their hearts, "Why does this fellow speak in this way? It is blasphemy! Who can forgive sins but God alone?" At once Jesus perceived in his spirit that they were discussing these questions among themselves; and he said to them, "Why do you raise such questions in your hearts? Which is easier, to say to the paralytic, 'Your sins are forgiven,' or to say, 'Stand up and walk'? But so that you may know that the Son of Man has authority on earth to forgive sins" - he said to the paralytic - "I say to you, stand up, take your mat and go to your home." And he stood up, and immediately took the mat and went out before all of them; so that they were all amazed and glorified God, saying, "We have never seen anything like this!"

Reader: The gospel of the Lord.
All: Praise to you, Lord Jesus Christ.

*Pause for silence.*

**The value of democracy stands or falls**
**with the values which it embodies and promotes.**
**Of course, values such as**
**the dignity of every human person,**
**respect for inviolable and inalienable human rights,**
**and the adoption of the "common good"**
**as the end and criterion regulating political life**
**are certainly fundamental and not to be ignored.**

The Gospel of Life (*Evangelium Vitae*), Pope John Paul II, 1995, #70

## December

# SABBATH REST

the right to trust in God

### I Heard The Voice Of Jesus

KINGSFOLD

1. I heard the voice of Je-sus say, "Come un-to me and rest;
2. I heard the voice of Je-sus say, "Be-hold, I free-ly give
3. I heard the voice of Je-sus say, "I am this dark world's light;

1. Lay down, you wea-ry one, lay down Your head up-on my breast."
2. The liv-ing wa-ter; thirst-y one, Stoop down, and drink and live."
3. Look un-to me, your morn shall rise And all your day be bright."

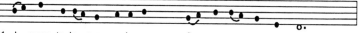

1. I came to Je-sus as I was, So wea-ry, worn and sad;
2. I came to Je-sus, and I drank Of that life-giv-ing stream.
3. I looked to Je-sus, and I found In him my star, my sun;

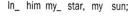

1. I found in him a rest-ing place, And he has made me glad.
2. My thirst was quenched, my soul re-vived, And now I live in him.
3. And in that light of life I'll walk, Till trav-'ling days are done.

Text: Horatius Bonar, 1808-1889, *Hymns Original and Selected*, 1846, adapted

Music: CMD, KINGSFOLD, traditional English Melody, adapted by Ralph Vaughan Williams, 1872-1958, 1906

*A tree gives glory to God by being a tree.*

Thomas Merton, *New Seeds of Contemplation*

## **OPENING PRAYER**

Leader: + O God, come to my assistance,

All: O Lord, make haste to help me.

Leader: Glory to the Father, and to the Son, and to the Holy Spirit,

All: As it was in the beginning, is now, and will be for ever. Amen.

## **PSALM 23**

Leader: The Lord has brought me to green pastures, alleluia.

*Side 1 (Leader's Side)*

The Lord is my shepherd, I shall not want.
He makes me lie down in green pastures;
he leads me beside still waters;
he restores my soul.

*Side 2*

He leads me in right paths
for his name's sake.
Even though I walk
through the darkest valley,
I fear no evil.

*1*

For you are with me;
your rod and your staff – they comfort me.
You prepare a table before me
in the presence of my enemies;
You anoint my head with oil;
my cup overflows.

<sup>2</sup>
Surely goodness and mercy shall follow me
all the days of my life,
and I shall dwell in the house of the Lord
my whole life long.

> <sup>1</sup>
> Glory to the Father, and to the Son,
> and to the Holy Spirit,
>
> <sup>2</sup>
> As it was in the beginning, is now,
> and will be for ever. Amen.

All
The Lord has brought me to green pastures,
alleluia.

## FIRST READING  2 Chronicles 36:15-17a,19-21

Reader: A reading from the second book of Chronicles.

The Lord, the God of their ancestors, sent persistently to them by his messengers, because he had compassion on his people and on his dwelling place; but they kept mocking the messengers of God, despising his words and scoffing at his prophets, until the wrath of the Lord against his people became so great that there was no remedy. Therefore he brought up against them the king of the Chaldeans, who…burned the house of God, broke down the wall of Jerusalem, burned its palaces with fire, and destroyed all its precious vessels. He took into exile in Babylon those who had escaped from the sword, and they became servants to him and to his sons until the establishment of the kingdom of Persia, to fulfill the word of the Lord by the mouth of Jeremiah, until the land had made up for its sabbaths. All the days that it lay desolate it kept sabbath, to fulfill seventy years.

Reader: The word of the Lord.
All: Thanks be to God.

## Psalm 42

Leader: My soul is thirsting for the living God.

1

As a deer longs for flowing streams,
so my soul longs for you, O God.
My soul thirsts for God,
for the living God.

2

When shall I come and behold
the face of God?
My tears have been my food day and night,
while people say to me continually,
"Where is your God?"

1

These things I remember,
as I pour out my soul:
how I went with the throng,
and led them in procession
to the house of God,
with glad shouts and songs of thanksgiving,
a multitude keeping festival.

2
Why are you cast down, O my soul,
and why are you disquieted within me?
Hope in God; for I shall again praise him,
my help and my God.

1
My soul is cast down within me;
therefore I remember you
from the land of Jordan and of Hermon,
from Mount Mizar.

2
Deep calls to deep
at the thunder of your cataracts;
all your waves and your billows
have gone over me.

1
By day the Lord commands his steadfast love,
and at night his song is with me,
a prayer to the God of my life.

2
I say to God, my rock,
"Why have you forgotten me?
Why must I walk about mournfully
because the enemy oppresses me?"

1
As with a deadly wound in my body,
my adversaries taunt me,
while they say to me continually,
"Where is your God?"

2
Why are you cast down, O my soul,
and why are you disquieted within me?
Hope in God; for I shall again praise him,
my help and my God.

<sup>1</sup>

Glory to the Father, and to the Son,
and to the Holy Spirit,

<sup>2</sup>

As it was in the beginning, is now,
and will be for ever. Amen.

All

My soul is thirsting for the living God.

## Psalm 146

Leader: I will praise my God all the days of my life.

<sup>1</sup>

Praise the Lord!
Praise the Lord, O my soul!
I will praise the Lord as long as I live;
I will sing praises to my God
all my life long.

<sup>2</sup>

Do not put your trust in princes,
in mortals, in whom there is no help.
When their breath departs,
they return to the earth;
on that very day their plans perish.

<sup>1</sup>

Happy are those
whose help is the God of Jacob,
whose hope is in the Lord their God,
who made heaven and earth,
the sea, and all that is in them;

<sup>2</sup>

Who keeps faith forever;
who executes justice for the oppressed;
who gives food to the hungry.

SABBATH REST

1
The Lord sets the prisoners free;
the Lord opens the eyes of the blind.
The Lord lifts up those who are bowed down;
the Lord loves the righteous.

2
The Lord watches over the strangers;
he upholds the orphan and the widow,
but the way of the wicked
he brings to ruin.

1
The Lord will reign forever,
your God, O Zion, for all generations.
Praise the Lord!

2
    Glory to the Father, and to the Son,
    and to the Holy Spirit,

1
    As it was in the beginning, is now,
    and will be for ever. Amen.

All
I will praise my God all the days of
my life.


## SECOND READING      1 Corinthians 11:23-26

Reader: A reading from the first letter of
       Paul to the Corinthians.

For I received from the Lord what I also
handed on to you, that the Lord Jesus on
the night when he was betrayed took a loaf
of bread, and when he had given thanks, he
broke it and said, "This is my body that is
for you. Do this in remembrance of me."
In the same way he took the cup also,

after supper, saying, "This cup is the new covenant in my blood. Do this, as often as you drink it, in remembrance of me." For as often as you eat this bread and drink this cup, you proclaim the Lord's death until he comes.

Reader: The word of the Lord.
All: Thanks be to God.

## PSALM 148

Leader: Praise the Lord from the heavens, alleuia.

1

Praise the Lord!
Praise the Lord from the heavens;
praise him in the heights!
Praise him, all his angels;
praise him, all his host!

2

Praise him, sun and moon;
praise him, all you shining stars!
Praise him, you highest heavens,
and you waters above the heavens!

1

Praise the Lord from the earth,
you sea monsters and all deeps,
fire and hail, snow and frost,
stormy wind fulfilling his command!

2

Mountains and all hills,
fruit trees and all cedars!
Wild animals and all cattle,
creeping things and flying birds!

1

Kings of the earth and all peoples,
princes and all rulers of the earth!
Young men and women alike,
old and young together!

2

Let them praise the name of the Lord,
for his name alone is exalted;
his glory is above earth and heaven.

1

He has raised up a horn for his people,
praise for all his faithful,
for the people of Israel
who are close to him.
Praise the Lord!

2

> Glory to the Father, and to the Son,
> and to the Holy Spirit,

1

> As it was in the beginning, is now,
> and will be for ever.  Amen.

All

Praise the Lord from the heavens, alleluia.


## THIRD READING

Mark 1:32-37

Reader: A reading from the gospel of Mark.

That evening, at sundown, they brought to
him all who were sick or possessed with
demons.  And the whole city was gathered
around the door.  And he cured many who
were sick with various diseases, and cast
out many demons; and he would not permit
the demons to speak, because they knew him.

In the morning, while it was still very dark, he got up and went out to a deserted place and there he prayed. And Simon and his companions hunted for him. When they found him, they said to him, "Everyone is searching for you."

Reader: The gospel of the Lord.
All: Praise to you, Lord Jesus Christ.

*Pause for silence.*

**These can be summed up as follows:**
**human life, as a gift of God, is sacred and inviolable...**
**Not only must human life not be taken,**
**but it must be protected with loving concern.**
**The meaning of life is found in giving and receiving love,**
**and in this light human sexuality and procreation**
**reach their true and full significance.**
**Love also gives meaning to suffering and death;**
**despite the mystery which surrounds them,**
**they can become saving events.**
**Respect for life requires that science and technology**
**should always be at the service of the human**
**and his or her integral development.**
**Society as a whole must respect, defend and promote**
**the dignity of every human person,**
**at every moment**
**and in every condition of that person's life.**

<u>The Gospel of Life</u> (*Evangelium Vitae*), Pope John Paul II, 1995, #81

## A Key Question?

*When is a human life a human person?*
*When are we talking about a soul?*

Some (claim) that the result of conception,
at least up to a certain number of days,
cannot yet be considered a personal human life.
But in fact,
"from the time that the ovum is fertilized, a life has begun
which is neither that of the father nor the mother;
it is rather the life of a new human being with his own growth.
It would never be made human if it were not human already.
This has always been clear,
and...modern genetic science offers clear confirmation.
It has determined that from the first instant there is established
the programme of what this living being will be:
a person, this individual person
with his(her) characteristic aspects already well determined.
Right from fertilization the adventure of human life begins,
and each of its capacities requires time - a rather lengthy time -
to find its place and to be in a position to act."   (CDF, 1974)
Even if the presence of a spiritual soul
cannot be ascertained by empirical data,
the results themselves of scientific research
on the human embryo provide
"a valuable indication for discerning by the use of reason
a personal presence at the moment
of the first appearance of a human life:   (CDF, 1988)
how could a human individual not be a human person?"
Furthermore, what is at stake is so important that,
from the standpoint of moral obligation,
the mere probability that a human person is involved
would suffice to justify an absolutely clear prohibition
of any intervention aimed at killing a human embryo...

The Gospel of Life (*Evangelium Vitae*), Pope John Paul II, 1995, #60

## Ponder Pages

I believe that everybody is pro-life about something. Two people may disagree about everything, or at least over all of the twelve "issues" offered for prayer in this little book. Even so, I believe that everybody is pro-life about something. The one friend who claimed to be pro-life about nothing admitted over lunch that there were ways of looking at many of these questions that he had simply not yet considered. He too is now pro-life, not yet about everything, but a willing work-in-process. Is that not a pretty good place to start?

If I am correct that everybody is pro-life about something, then have we not an outstanding opportunity to join forces, or as St. Paul would say, to "build up" one another, as the body of Christ, as the people of God, into a coalition of justice, peace, and mercy in the social and economic and, yes, even in the political? Since the beginning, the Church has sought to pray, study, act, and love.

Let me presume to offer some thoughts on each of these issues, with a little room for your own thoughts and notes. Please, do not take these ponderings as a substitute for the encyclical itself.

### THE ADOPTION OPTION
If people dealing with unexpected pregnancies knew what I have heard in the sacrament of reconciliation and in pastoral counseling about the long-term suffering of the mothers and fathers, abortions would indeed be rare. And I don't know why the abortion clinics are not being sued for withholding information about the physical and psychological damage done to parents.


### HEALTH CARE WITH DIGNITY
I do not know why health care should be available only to people who are fortunate enough to have the right kind of job, nor does it make sense to expose any family to bankruptcy just because someone is sick.


### NONVIOLENCE OF JESUS
I stay frustrated with the disconnect of Christians between today's death penalty and the crucifixion of Jesus Christ. The idea that we have to kill people who kill people to show that killing people is wrong is itself wrong, and insane.

## God's Good Earth

The earth is a gift to us from God which we will pass on to God's children coming after us. To deplete the gardens of God's earth to make money to spend today is at minimum theft from the future, and possibly murder of our future.

## Work That Works

If I hire a full-time worker, and expect him or her to work for me full-time, then he or she is earning a living wage, even if I do not pay a living wage. If I pay less than a living wage because I can get away with it, then I am saying to the rest of the community that they have an obligation to subsidize my enterprise through taxes or charity. What makes it immoral is the undignified way this system treats lowest paid workers.

## BEING SEXUAL BEINGS

The statistic is that more people lose their virginity in the month of June than in any other month. Sexuality is a gift from God that brings us together as human beings. Human sexuality is not entirely genital, nor is it meant to be. Still it may be (as one good friend puts it) God's greatest joke on us. It is also a fire that can burn us. As I say to the teens, if you're not ready to bring a child into this world, and deal with that life-changing event, then you're not ready for you-know-what, and if you don't know "what" I'm talking about, let's talk.

## FREEDOM OF RELIGION

Many Americans are uncomfortable about it, but even in our imperfect ways we have given the world a witness to how peoples of different religions and faiths can live side by side with tolerance and even respect. Throughout history, religious peoples have sought to make their presence felt through government. When they have succeeded, the results have often been catastrophic.

## Food, Clothing and Shelter

In the Hebrew ethic, society is judged by how the widows, the aliens and the orphans are faring. We are indeed called to do our best to build economic, social and political systems of justice. But there will always be people who fall through the cracks. This is when charity becomes necessary.

## Education

Education is one of the established rights of each human being. The people who have the capacity to improve education are most of the very people who no longer need it. If those with the power and means worry only about the education of their own, we risk forgetting that all children are with us brothers and sisters in Christ.

## Natural Dying

The process of dying is proclaimed by some as our greatest fear. Perhaps we all want to avoid the pain. The priesthood has shown me that the greatest consolation to a dying person is the awareness that he or she has loved and is still being loved. While we are blessed with medicine and facilities that can help to minimize pain,

no drug can equal the consolation of love.
None of us is a machine with a humanly
determinable "useful" life.

## WORLD PEACE

Every time we have to resort to war,
it means we have failed again as human
beings. The temptation of war is that
it can seem a simple matter of naming an
enemy and attacking. The difficulty of
making and sustaining peace can be those
unpredictable details hard to measure.
Eventually, the only path to peace is
the one Jesus gives: forgiveness.

## SABBATH REST

If I never take a sabbath day of rest,
sooner or later something unhealthy is
going to happen. Even trumping physical
and mental health, if I never take a day
of rest then am I not trying to be God?
Or am I saying that God is not doing
a good enough job? Just watching the
world around me, the stress caused by
lack of free time is squeezing the very
life out of us.